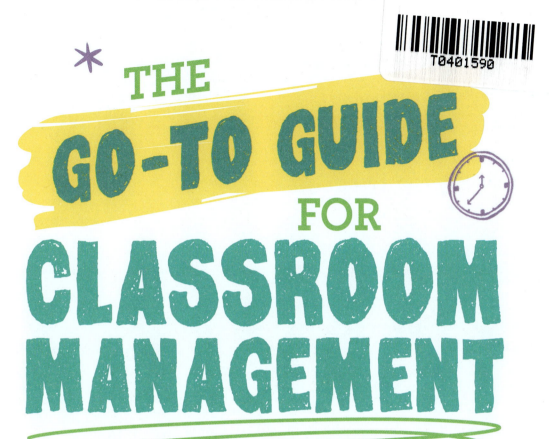

THE GO-TO GUIDE FOR CLASSROOM MANAGEMENT

Quick Tips, Effective Strategies, and Use-Now Tools for Teaching Success

Created in collaboration with the Scholastic Teacher Fellows

JENNIFER L. W. FINK

To Eddie, Hannah, Tiffany—
without you, this book wouldn't exist.

Senior Vice President and Publisher: Tara Welty
Editorial Director: Sarah Longhi
Editor-in-Chief: Raymond Coutu
Production Editor: Danny Miller
Assistant Editor: Samantha Unger
Editorial Assistant: Ella Wertz
Creative Director: Tannaz Fassihi
Cover Design: Cynthia Ng
Interior Design: Maria Lilja
Doodle Art: Tanya Chernyak

Photos ©: cover: Scholastic Inc.; 6–8: Bianca Alexis. All other photos © Courtesy of Scholastic Teacher Fellows.

Credits: 23, 55(t): Pages from *Classroom Fitness Breaks to Help Kids Focus* text copyright © 2011 by Sarah Longhi, illustrations by Brian LaRossa copyright © 2011 by Scholastic Inc. Used by permission; 55(b): *Brain Breaks for the Classroom* by Michelle Gay with photography by Maria Lilja and Rondell Romiel copyright © 2009 by Scholastic Inc.; 56: *The Scholastic Teacher Plan Book* by Bill Singer and Tonya Ward Singer with illustrations by Kate Flanagan copyright © 2005 by Scholastic Inc.; 60: *Daily Word Ladders: Content Areas: Grades 2–3* and *Grades 4–6* text copyright © 2019 by Timothy V. Rasinski and Melissa Cheesman Smith, photography by Kelly Kennedy copyright © 2019 by Scholastic Inc. Used by permission; 96: *Scholastic News Sticky Situation Cards: Grades 1–3* and *Grades 4–6* text and illustrations copyright © 2021 by Scholastic Inc. All rights reserved.

ISBN 978-1-5461-7158-4

1 2 3 4 5 6 7 8 9 10   40   34 33 32 31 30 29 28 27 26 25

Scholastic Inc., 557 Broadway, New York, NY 10012

CONTENTS

SCHOLASTIC TEACHER FELLOWS

Each year, the Scholastic Teacher Fellows program brings together 18 kindergarten through eighth-grade educators from across the country to help solve pressing teacher challenges—like classroom management—through action research and collaborative resource design. Throughout this book, you'll see a number of ideas and visual contributions from these 18 brilliant educators, whose support made this book possible.

"The things we do in the classroom can have a positive impact for generations to come."

—VALENTE' GIBSON, afterschool coordinator

Sherri Amos is a fourth-grade teacher at Copeland Elementary School in Augusta, Georgia, with eight years of experience teaching first through fourth grades.

Alexandra Felix is a second-grade teacher at P.S. 122 The Mamie Fay School in Astoria, Queens, with 10 years of experience supporting English Language Learners.

BreAnn Fennell is a third-grade teacher at Reagan Elementary School in Ashland, Ohio, with 14 years of experience as a classroom teacher.

Kevin Frederick is a first-grade teacher at South Side School in Champaign, Illinois, with 12 years of experience as a classroom teacher.

Valente' Gibson is an afterschool coordinator who previously taught third grade at Jackson Creek Elementary School in Columbia, South Carolina. He has eight years of experience teaching third and fifth grades.

Grace Hearl is a sixth-grade teacher at East Rockford Middle School in Rockford, Michigan, with five years of experience teaching ELA and social studies.

Bridget Jordan is a first- and fourth-grade ESOL teacher at Baltimore Highlands Elementary School in Baltimore, Maryland, with five years of experience supporting English Language Learners.

Katie Kim is a fifth-grade teacher at Warner Avenue Elementary School in Los Angeles, California, with three years of experience as a classroom teacher and as an Intervention Specialist.

Paul King is a sixth-grade social-studies teacher at Global Village Academy North in Thornton, Colorado. He has 10 years of experience in Colorado, Costa Rica, and Taiwan.

 Hannah Kittle is a fifth-grade teacher at Joseph A. Browne Middle School in Chelsea, Massachusetts, with 10 years of experience as an educator across diverse K–12 learning environments.

 Morgan Mercado is a third-grade teacher at Dr. Raphael A. Baranco Elementary School in Lafayette Parish, Louisiana, with eight years of experience teaching third- and fourth-grade gifted students.

 Michele Ogden is a third-grade teacher at Solis Park K–8 School in Irvine, California, with 10 years of experience as an educator and former elementary school principal.

 Melanie Okadigwe is a PreK through sixth-grade Learning Specialist at Greene Hill School in Brooklyn, New York, with 19 years of experience as an educator across diverse learning environments.

 Keke Powell is a second-grade teacher at Sunfield Elementary School in Buda, Texas, with 10 years of experience teaching second through fifth grades in Hawaii and Texas.

 Milagros Sanchez-Cohen is a kindergarten teacher at Horeb Christian School in Hialeah, Florida, with 13 years of experience as a classroom teacher.

 Eddie Vitcavage is a fifth-grade teacher at Roger Sherman Elementary School in Meriden, Connecticut, with four years of experience as a classroom teacher.

 Tim Wheeler is a third-grade teacher at Williams Elementary School in Mattoon, Illinois, with seven years of experience teaching third- and fourth-grade students.

 Tiffany Young-Norris is a kindergarten teacher at C.T. Walker Magnet School in Augusta, Georgia, with 10 years of experience teaching PreK and English as a Second Language to K–12 students.

"Be kind to yourself and give yourself grace. You can't do it all."
—KEVIN FREDERICK, first-grade teacher

SCHOLASTIC

TEACHER FELLOWS

Scan this QR code to learn more about the Scholastic Teacher Fellows program and how you can apply to make a difference.

INTRODUCTION

TEACHERS LOVE CLIFFORD, THE BIG RED DOG.

That's one of my takeaways from the 2024 Scholastic Teacher Fellows Summit, where I had the pleasure of meeting that year's Teacher Fellows, a diverse group of amazing educators from across the United States.

They'd come to New York City to share their expertise and insights with Scholastic publishing teams—and with me, an education journalist who was tasked with helping them bring one of their ideas to life: a new book to help teachers navigate classroom management.

Behavior challenges, disengaged students, and underdeveloped social skills are increasingly common in K–12 classrooms. We are still feeling the impact of the COVID-19 pandemic in

schools. Chronic absenteeism is up—along with classroom disruptions and disrespect, according to a 2024 survey by the National Center for Education Statistics. Eight out of 10 public school leaders say that the pandemic and its lingering effects continue to negatively impact students' socio-emotional and behavioral development.

These stats echo what the Teacher Fellows told us: Teachers—especially new ones—need tools to help with classroom management. Hannah Kittle, a fifth-grade teacher from Massachusetts, summed it up like this: "If you can't manage your classroom, you can't teach."

So we collaborated to create this tool: *The Go-To Guide for Classroom Management*. It's an easy-to-use handbook built on lived teacher experience and solid research.

Teacher Fellows meet Clifford in person!

The strategies the Teacher Fellows shared with me overlap with some of the key evidence-based classroom management strategies recommended by the National Council on Teacher Quality (NCTQ, 2020):

* Establish rules and routines.
* Maximize learning time.
* Reinforce positive behavior.
* Redirect off-task behavior.

And here's the best part: Implementing the tips shared in this book can make education a more joyful—and productive—experience for you and your students. Positive teacher-student relationships increase teacher well-being and student connectedness to school, which can increase academic achievement. According to the NCTQ, students learn 20% more when their teachers create a positive classroom environment.

This book will show you how.

WHO THIS BOOK IS FOR

Any current or prospective K–6 educator: i.e., teachers in training; new teachers (including just-out-of-college teachers and those transitioning to education from another career); teacher coaches and mentors; and any educator who wants to boost their classroom management skills.

As a teacher, you are on the frontlines—often in undersourced settings with too little support—working with the children who will shape our collective future. And because you know it is mission-critical, you show up, strategize, and shepherd our children.

Thank you!

This book will help you create a safe, secure learning environment that will allow you and your students to thrive.

Jennifer

P.S. I love Clifford, too.

HOW TO USE THIS BOOK

However you'd like! You can read it front to back, or you can go straight to the section that addresses your current classroom management concerns. Or you can flip it open at random for a quick hit of inspiration and fresh ideas.

CHOOSE AMONG THESE THREE PARTS

Go here for help establishing structure and standards.

PART 1: ROUTINES & NORMS
Creating a Safe, Sane Classroom

Explore strategies for making the most of class time and classroom space.

PART 2: TIME & SPACE
Organizing Daily Classroom Life

Discover how to build strong relationships with students, families, and colleagues.

PART 3: RELATIONSHIPS
Nurturing Connections & Building Confidence

There are many ways to capture your thoughts and ideas as you read. You might:

- flag pages with sticky notes.
- make notes in the margins.
- use a notebook or app to expand on questions, prompts, and exercises throughout the book.

There's power in sharing ideas, too, so think about organizing a formal or informal book study with colleagues.

Collaborating makes your professional life more manageable (and a lot more fun)!

WATCH FOR THESE RECURRING FEATURES

Teacher Toolbox
Practical tips to help you succeed in the classroom

Images from real classrooms
Peek into the Teacher Fellows' classrooms for sage advice and new ideas.

Spotlight on...
Teacher-tested strategies you can use to involve and engage students

Book recommendations
Learn more with suggested titles.

Did you know?
Research tidbits that highlight the key ideas and strategies in a section

Think
Key questions to consider for your own classroom

QR codes
Access additional information, worksheets, and teacher-created videos by scanning the included codes with the QR reader on your phone.

Connect & Reflect
Interactive activities to help you apply what you've learned to your teaching practice

PART 1

ROUTINES & NORMS

CREATING A SAFE, SANE CLASSROOM

Chaos might be the first word that comes to mind if you peek into Tim Wheeler's third-grade classroom in October. Students are out of their seats, moving around the room. A few kids are sprawled on the floor. Two are huddled under the classroom sink. Kids' voices rise and fall.

At first, you can't even see Tim. But when you look closer, you notice him crouched on the floor, giving feedback to three children working on a writing assignment. You notice open notebooks, enthusiastic conversations, and concentrated effort. Students are on task and engaged. What initially looked like chaos is actually productive, directed energy and action.

That's *not* what Tim's classroom looked like on Day 1—not on the first day of the school year and definitely not on his first day as a teacher. It took time for him and his class to develop (and practice) the routines and norms that help them work in harmony.

As Tim's students master basic routines, he offers them more choice, as with their writing workspaces.

LET'S BEGIN

Ideally, you're thinking about your daily plan and classroom climate even before the beginning of the school year, since you'll want to introduce basic routines and start talking about norms with students right from the start. But you also may be in the midst of a challenging year, ready to get more strategic.

No matter the situation, this section will help you think about what you want your class to look like, feel like, and sound like:

* When students enter the room
* During instructional time
* During work time
* During transitions

Taking time to picture and play out each scenario helps you design routines and expectations that work for you.

RULE OF THUMB: Investing time NOW to create and teach (or improve!) routines and norms pays off in more time for teaching content LATER.

In this section, you'll learn:

✩ **What classroom routines to prioritize**

✩ **How to craft and teach routines effectively**

✩ **Why routines matter for your well-being**

✩ **How to co-create a class contract**

✩ **How to help students apply class norms**

✩ **When to review class routines and norms**

OUR CLASSROOM
Constitution

We the students of this class, in order to form a more perfect classroom, will follow the following rules:

1. Keep hands to yourself
2. Be respectful and kind
3. Listen to the teacher
4. Be an Alaka'i
5. Have fun

We declare this for our class of <u>2nd</u> grade at our school, <u>Sunfield Elementary</u>
x <u>G203 Alaka'i</u>

Keke Powell's second graders co-create their class constitution, laying the ground rules for a respectful classroom community. Keke teaches them Alaka'i, the Hawaiian word for leader or guide.

ROUTINES

ROUTINES 101

You've probably heard it before: Routines can be the difference between your ability to teach what you've planned—or not! Routines are know-by-heart tasks that increase students' time on task and keep the classroom running smoothly, without your constant oversight.

Classroom routines also:

✳ Increase student engagement

✳ Decrease disruptive behavior

✳ Boost student independence

✳ Promote a peaceful learning environment

✳ Help you meet diverse academic, social, and behavioral needs

Did you know…?
Daily routines have been shown to free up cognitive capacity for problem-solving; when educators spend less time thinking or worrying about the dozens of repeatable tasks they and their students do, everyone in the class saves mental energy for learning and applying that learning (DaSilva, 2023).

"Picture this: You want to design a lesson where students will work in pairs to jot ideas on sticky notes. Do you have a system for partnering up at desks? On the rug? How will sticky notes and pencils get distributed swiftly? The more routines we teach our students to handle recurring tasks, the more effective our teaching can be."

—MORGAN MERCADO, third-grade teacher

ESTABLISH EVERYDAY ROUTINES

It's up to you to decide which routines you want to establish. Think about the activities your students need to do on a regular basis—everything from entering the classroom to turning in work, using the restroom, and sharpening a pencil. Explicitly outlining the specific steps you'd like your students to follow when they do these tasks will set them up for success.

"Teach everything; assume nothing."

—KEVIN FREDERICK, first-grade teacher

Common everyday routines include:

★ Entering the classroom
★ Visiting the bathroom
★ Moving through school
★ Dismissing students at the end of the day

You'll also need routines for:

★ Emergency drills
★ Classroom visitors
★ Use of classroom materials

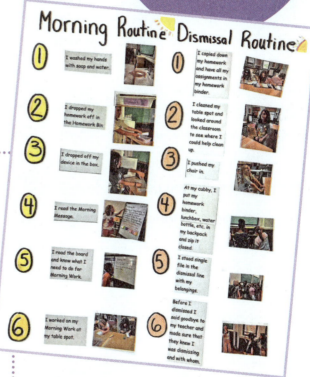

Students love to see themselves featured on this routines poster created by Melanie Okadigwe's colleague, fifth-grade teacher Liu Volpe. The photos reinforce desirable behaviors for everyone!

 THINK What activities will your students do each day or on a recurring schedule?

Here is a list of common classroom routines. Check the boxes that apply to your classroom for each routine in the list.

DOWNLOAD HERE!

 ## PUTTING ROUTINES INTO ACTION

Common Classroom Routine	I have a routine	I need a routine	Not applicable
Entering the classroom			
Gaining the teacher's attention			
Going to the restroom			
Passing out materials			
Sharing materials with peers			
Using classroom materials			
Completing independent work			
Completing group work			
Preparing for homework assignments			
Turning in assignments			
Sharpening pencils			
Leaving the classroom			
Using books from the classroom library			
Playing on the playground			
Other:			

PLANNING ROUTINES

Time to start planning some routines! Remember that a routine that works for first graders probably won't work for fifth graders. And the routines used by the veteran teacher down the hall might not work for you. The most effective routines are tailored to the needs of your class. When crafting routines, think about:

* **Administrative requirements.** Your school may have specific guidelines that all teachers need to follow during lockdown or fire drills, for instance. The administration may also have specific rules that govern student behavior in the halls or at recess.

* **Student development.** Routines must be developmentally appropriate. Younger kids can't sit still or be quiet for prolonged periods of time; older students crave independence.

* **Your preferences.** If you don't like the routine, you are unlikely to reinforce it. Inject a little bit of fun—and a bit of your personality—into your routines. (Love music? Consider playing music in the background as students enter the room.)

* **Student needs and preferences.** You might not know much about your students before Day 1, but as you get to know them, don't hesitate to tweak class routines in response to their likes, dislikes, and needs.

* **Priorities.** What is the most important thing you want a particular routine to accomplish? Health and safety, of course, are top priorities. Tim Wheeler says his number one objective is "getting his class where they need to be" when they move through the halls, so he doesn't stress out if students whisper to one another.

Successful routines target a consistent, necessary action you or your students do as part of the school day and are composed of a series of simple, repeatable steps.

"My students love to chant and move, so we use a lot of classroom chants in my classroom throughout the day—from lining up to focusing before a lesson. Our chants keep our classroom lives in order and help my students to be successful."

—KEKE POWELL,
second-grade teacher

SPOTLIGHT ON ROUTINES

START CLASS ON A POSITIVE NOTE!

Greetings!

Keep morning greetings both low-prep and fun by allowing students to select a greeting that is just right for them each day. Create a visual with several greeting options (hug, high five, fist bump, etc.) and post it outside of your door. Each day, students can choose how they'd like to be greeted before they enter your classroom. Alternately (or later in the year), you might ask students to create their own handshake/greeting to celebrate their unique personalities.

GOOD MORNING, FRIENDS!

CHOOSE A MORNING GREETING!

HUG

HIGH FIVE

FIST BUMP

PEACE SIGN

WAVE

Alexandra Felix's second graders get to share a friendly greeting of their choice with her each day.

Our Morning Routine

Put away bookbag

Take out orange folder and put in mailbox

Make lunch choice

Take book box or sketch pad to your desk

Draw or read quietly

Listen for instructions

Unpacking and Setting Up

After their special greeting, help students transition calmly into the room with an easy-to-remember sequence of steps to put belongings away and to get ready for the first activity. This sequence could include unpacking homework and other materials, sharpening pencils, turning in forms, and more. A list of what students must do should be posted in a spot they can see clearly when they arrive.

It will take time (and lots of practice!) for students to master this routine, but when they do, you'll be able to carry out your morning responsibilities as your learners manage theirs.

Kevin Frederick uses pictures paired with short directives to support his first-grade readers.

Morning Work at Your Desk

Having a short, daily task for students eases them into learning and targets key skills they may use during the day. (It also frees you up to greet and check in with students individually.) Morning work should:

* ✳ Activate students' prior learning to review all the skills they're building
* ✳ Take only 3–5 minutes
* ✳ Be completed silently and independently
* ✳ Be easily accessible to students to ensure independence

Name: _____   204   208   209   217

I can analyze, in speaking and writing, the setting of The Breadwinner and how it impacts the characters by annotating and using adjectives.

What is it like where Parvana lives? Collect examples.

What words would you use to describe the setting? Use at least 2 - 3 adjectives.

Hannah Kittle's fifth graders have a five-minute ELA assignment waiting on their desks each morning. Their responses help Hannah check for understanding.

SIGNALS SAVE THE DAY!

Create nonverbal signals to cue routines and expectations, especially during independent work time. Simple nonverbal cues can reduce distractions, too.

* ✳ **Volume Signals** Use a striking visual cue, such as a chart with four large button lights, each matched to a different volume level. Turn on the light that's appropriate for a given activity as a visual reminder of what volume is expected.

* ✳ **Hand Signals** Familiar hand signals can help you quickly address students and give them permission to proceed without missing a beat. For instance, a student might hold up one finger for getting water, and you might give a thumbs-up in response when you're meeting with a small group.

Without saying a word, Eddie Vitcavage can signal his fifth graders to speak at an appropriate volume.

MORNING ROUTINES

Think about what you can do to help mornings get off to a good start. Here are some ideas:

Be a Tone-Setter

Students will read your energy from a distance. Be ready to greet them at the classroom door or wherever you pick them up. Think of welcoming expressions that feel authentic to you—do you like to smile serenely, make heart-hands, or sing a short verse? Choose something to let each child know that you are present for them and happy to have them at school.

Keke Powell sometimes dresses up to match her door decor! This back-to-school door introduces some of the Hawaiian words her second graders will be learning, as well as a "good character" writing prompt: "Stand tall and wear a crown" (like a pineapple!).

Morning Meeting

Gathering with your class each morning is a wonderful way to build community, prepare students for the day ahead, and quickly take attendance or lunch count. Start with a brief attention-grabbing game, such as following different clapping rhythms, or with an engaging question related to a topic you're studying (e.g., Would you rather explore a tundra or a grassland?). Give them a rundown of what to expect for the day; review the schedule and answer any questions they may have. Make sure that all students have what they need to be successful for the day, and you're off to a great start.

At morning meeting, Milagros Sanchez-Cohen invites kindergartners up to the whiteboard for calendar math.

Connect & Reflect

Use the planner to sketch out your own morning routine.

DOWNLOAD HERE!

☑ ROUTINE PLANNER

How will you greet your students each morning?	**Example:** I'll stand at the door and give every student a high-five as they enter.
What do students need to unpack?	**Example:** Book, homework folder
Where do students put their materials?	**Example:** <u>On desk</u>: Book, homework, notebook for morning work, sharpened pencil. <u>In desk</u>: Homework folder
Where can students get the supplies they will need for the day?	**Example:** Extra pencils and paper at student self-serve station; books in book bins
What housekeeping tasks do I need to complete in the morning?	**Example:** I'll take attendance and give announcements for the day.
When and how will I complete them?	**Example:** During arrival/morning work
How will I practice and reinforce arrival and dismissal expectations with students?	**Example:** I'll explain and demonstrate. We'll practice, review, and practice again throughout the first weeks.

ESTABLISHING ROUTINES

Introducing routines is often the easy part. Teaching routines takes time, determination, and patience. A sense of humor helps, too! Laughing about mishaps and misunderstandings is healthier than obsessing and stressing—and helps your students understand that mistakes are both a part of life and a learning opportunity. (See page 81 for motivating ways to talk about mistakes with your class.)

These three tips can help:

1 **Be clear.** Detail what you want your students to do.

- **Vague:** *Get ready and line up.*
- **Better:** *Wait for my hand signal to line up. Find your spot. Hands to yourself. Whisper voices.*

2 **Model.** Show your students what you want them to do. Have fun with it! Over-exaggerate your actions. Purposely do it "wrong" (after you've demonstrated the right way) and let your students point out your mistakes.

3 **Practice, practice, practice!** Repetition is key to establishing routines. Adding challenges is one way to maintain student engagement. Consider timing how long it takes your students to line up, for instance, and challenge them to do it quicker next time.

"Initially, you have to be very specific about what you're looking for. As students practice and learn routines, they will be able to act independently without even thinking about it."

—EDDIE VITCAVAGE,
fifth-grade teacher

Watch this!

Paul King's sixth graders and Keke Powell's second graders snap to attention when their teachers use these clever cues to start a lesson.

GRADUAL RELEASE OF RESPONSIBILITY

The Gradual Release of Responsibility (GRR) is a classroom management strategy that helps you gradually shift responsibility for learning to your students (Fisher & Frey, 2015). It involves four stages:

1 **Modeling (*I Do, You Watch*)** The teacher demonstrates the classroom routine and shares aloud any internal thinking that may be helpful to support student understanding.

2 **Guided practice (*You Do, I Help*)** The teacher and students practice the skill together. The teacher provides feedback specific to the task and thinking processes.

3 **Collaborative practice (*You Do, We Help*)** Students work together to practice the skill with peer and teacher support. The teacher may ask students to remember what they learned through previous attempts and act on what was learned.

4 **Independent practice (*You Do, We Celebrate*)** Students practice the skill on their own, and the teacher provides positive praise and opportunities for celebration when routines are completed successfully.

NOTE: This strategy can be applied to anything you teach!

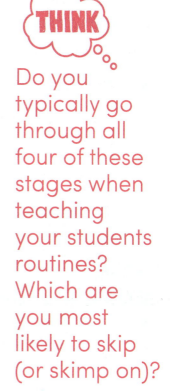

THINK

Do you typically go through all four of these stages when teaching your students routines? Which are you most likely to skip (or skimp on)?

How Long Will It Take?

It typically takes a couple of months for classroom routines to become second nature. If you start school in September, expect things to be running smoothly by late November. Until then, keep practicing!

GRR IN ACTION: LINING UP AND WALKING DOWN THE HALL

1 I Do, You Watch

Be specific and visual! Demonstrate and narrate in detail your expectations, including how to:

* Get up from the table/desk (e.g., pushing in the chairs, taking any needed materials)

* Walk to the line calmly

* Keep a safe distance from the person in front of you

* Watch where you're going, and keep up the pace

* Keep to the right in the hall

* Watch for signals to start/stop/pause

* Give themselves reminders and cues (e.g., "I'll say to myself, 'I need to keep my voice quiet, so I don't disturb other classes.'")

Younger students might learn best with a song or chant attached to each step.

2 You Do, I Help

Now invite students to try it, and ask them to narrate what they're doing in their heads. (Have one or two students narrate out loud so the class can hear them.) Have them pause if they missed a step, and prompt them to do a retake on their own, reminding them of the steps as needed. Be sure to thank students for recognizing missed steps for the class, so you emphasize that fixing mistakes is a natural way to learn.

Watch the catchy chants and gestures kindergarten teacher Milagros Sanchez-Cohen and second-grade teacher Keke Powell use to engage their students and cue them to walk in the halls quickly and quietly.

❸ You Do, We Help

Invite a group of students to demonstrate a routine and encourage feedback from the rest of the students who are observing how their peers did it. You might say, "Let's see Table 3 model how to line up and walk in the hallway. I'll need help from the class to give Table 3 some feedback." After students are done, encourage a round of applause (or jazz hands or snaps of appreciation!). Then ask the students watching to give compliments about what worked and suggestions for improvements that everyone can try together.

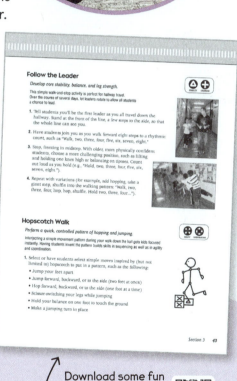

❹ You Do, We Celebrate

Challenge students to apply all the skills they've learned in real time. "All right, everyone, it's that time! Time to transition to lunch. Let's put into practice everything we've discussed about walking in the hallway. I'm excited to see each of you demonstrating what we've talked about. And remember, when you see me give the A-OK sign, you'll know that I see you doing exactly what's expected. Let's head out to lunch smoothly and safely!"

ONGOING REINFORCEMENT

Let students know how much you value their attention to keeping a routine running smoothly. For example, once students are walking smoothly (or to incentivize them to do so), you can add some fun physical challenges.

Download some fun ways to give kids a chance to move more and focus!

Connect & Reflect

How can you apply the Gradual Release of Responsibility strategy to teach students a new routine?
Use the space below to brainstorm.

DOWNLOAD HERE!

☑ **APPLY THE GRR TO TEACH ROUTINES**

Gradual Release of Responsibility (GRR) Routine:	
I Do, You Watch	
You Do, I Help	
You Do, We Help	
You Do, We Celebrate	

WHAT TO DO WHEN KIDS AREN'T GETTING IT

See next page for more ideas about giving rewards, or not!

Identify and Address Obstacles

Try simplifying the routine. Consider asking students why they're having a difficult time or, as Tim Wheeler asks, "What could have gone better?" You may be surprised at their insight!

Practice

If students are struggling, practice with them apart from their peers. That can open up the opportunity for a student to become an "expert" in the target routine or skill. The outcome? A chance for the student to gain confidence by helping peers with a task they once struggled with.

Chart Progress

Involve your students in measuring and documenting their growth. Concrete evidence of improvement is motivating (for both you and your students!).

FOCUS ON THE POSITIVE

Drawing attention to what students are doing wrong won't help. Instead, praise and reinforce what they're doing *right*. Positive reinforcement is the most effective way to teach new behavior.

"I say things like, 'There's a lot to like here! Almost everyone in our group met ALL the expectations. Let's talk about what went right.'"

—TIM WHEELER,
third-grade teacher

For the most challenging routines, it's a good idea to hang picture-based posters at eye level to help students self-monitor. (These posters were created by Melanie Okadigwe's colleague, first-grade teacher Anthony Bradfield.)

BreAnn Fennell posts messages to remind kids of morning tasks they are learning to do independently.

TO REWARD OR NOT TO REWARD?

You may have heard that giving students rewards for desired behavior decreases internal motivation or erodes students' natural love of learning. If you haven't, you'll likely encounter that line of thinking sooner or later, perhaps from a parent or colleague. But the bulk of evidence suggests that external awards do not destroy intrinsic motivation (Archer & Hughes, 2010).

Did you know...?
Rewarding students with privileges—like lunch with you, the opportunity to wear a hat or sit with a friend—can build relationships, too (Bear & Minke, 2018).

Class-based reward systems and token economies can make learning and practicing routines fun, especially if you keep these tips in mind.

DO	DON'T
Use rewards selectively. Celebrate students' successes in areas that need reinforcement.	Use rewards to shame students who have not yet met the criteria.
Tailor rewards to individual progress. Consider when individual recognition or reward systems may be more appropriate than group rewards or privileges. Work any individual system out with both the student and their family so everyone is on the same page.	Set up a system without some way of tracking the progress, such as a daily chart each week you or students can mark.
Reward students fairly. Clearly communicate the criteria for earning rewards and apply them consistently.	Promise something you can't deliver or is too complicated to deliver consistently.
Taper rewards as the desired behavior emerges. As students get better at a behavior, start spacing out your praise and rewards—a technique psychologists call "fading." The goal is to help students internalize the behavior.	Give rewards and praise all the time once a routine is learned. Rewards (and praise) are most effective when given every so often.

Simple, Cheap, Non-Food Rewards

Students love treats! But because all students and families have unique dietary needs (including allergies and faith-based restrictions), it's best to avoid food-based rewards. Here are some alternatives:

❋ **Award coupons.** Reward your students with coupons they can redeem for privileges, such as extra free time.

❋ **Class experiences.** How about letting your students select some music to play during work time? Or scheduling a sing-along?

❋ **Trinkets.** Think fun erasers, special pencils, and stickers. Don't overdo it, though. A little goes a long way—and fun fact: even older students love collecting stickers.

❋ **Public recognition.** Celebrate your students. You can honor them with a classroom display or give them a shout-out in morning announcements.

Here are some ready-to-go coupons for easy-to-implement rewards, such as being Teacher's Helper for a day.

Token Economies

A classroom token economy is a management system used to reinforce positive behavior and reward progress. Students earn tokens (such as points, "Class Cash," or chips) when they display certain behaviors or meet goals. Students can exchange their tokens later for rewards and privileges—and usually, they end up building their math skills and economic awareness as well!

ROAR Drawing Prizes

Lunch Bunch (5)
Desk Pet
Sticker Store
Pencil Store
Eraser Store
Add a Song
Pick the Read Aloud
Class Stuffy for the Day

Michele Ogden's students enjoy receiving ROAR cards from any adult in the school who notices their great work or behavior. Michele draws one or more cards each day (especially at the beginning of the year). Students whose cards are picked can choose from any of the ROAR prizes in class (see poster).

PRIORITIZING YOUR NEEDS

It's easy to get swept up in your **students' needs**, but if you don't schedule time to care for *your* physical **and mental** well-being, you'll burn out. You'll be a healthier, **happier, more** effective teacher if you build in some "me time."

Did you know...?
Your brain actually shrinks when you're even mildly dehydrated. That can cause you to forget things and have trouble focusing and making decisions. In general, about 20% of the water people consume comes from foods and other liquids—in addition to this, setting a goal of eight or more cups of water a day can help you think clearly and keep calm (Mayo Clinic, 2023).

"You cannot pour from an empty cup. Taking care of yourself is imperative for a successful school year!"

—TIFFANY YOUNG-NORRIS,
kindergarten teacher

Healthy habits support well-being, but making time for them can be challenging! Here's how veteran teachers build them into their daily and weekly routines:

✻ Hydration

Drinking **enough water** is vital to your body and brain functioning at an optimal level. Fifth-grade teacher Eddie Vitcavage makes sure his **48-ounce water bottle** is full before class starts, sips on it throughout the morning, refills it at lunch, and finishes it over the afternoon. (Don't like plain water? A lot of teachers use flavor or vitamin packets to bump up the taste.)

✻ Bathroom Breaks

Yes, there are real health risks to "holding it" (including raising your anxiety!) during long stretches of instruction. Make it a priority to arrange a consistent time with an instructional aide, coach, or the teacher next door to supervise your class—a predictable break can make a big difference (and you can return the favor!).

✳ Nutrition

Food is fuel. You need enough protein, carbs, and healthy fats to function your best—just like your students do! Tim packs his lunches the night before—right after dinner is ideal, he says, because "it's easier to make healthy choices on a full stomach."

✳ Exercise

"I use exercise as a coping mechanism to unwind and de-stress," says fifth-grade teacher Hannah Kittle. "Exercise is a chance to turn your brain off for the day."

Tiffany uses exercise to fuel her day, "I wake up early each morning and participate in a spin class. This sets the tone for my day, helping me to begin energized and ready for my students." BreAnn Fennell does coach-led workouts.

✳ Sleep

Your body and mind need at least seven hours of sleep each night. Having a hard time shutting down your thoughts? Heed Kevin's advice: "Give yourself permission to completely shut off from work-related tasks."

If it helps, remind yourself that sleep will help you problem-solve and handle tomorrow's conflicts with grace.

THINK

What happens when you're short on sleep? When you haven't gotten enough physical activity or time with friends? Think about how prioritizing your physical, mental, and emotional well-being will boost your ability to create a supportive learning environment and effectively engage with your students.

✳ Social Interaction

In times of high stress, we often withdraw from those around us. But human interaction is essential for our well-being. So build in time with family and friends. ("Make peace with the idea that you may have to be the one to reach out," Tim says.) You might not *think* you have time for coffee with a friend, but you may ultimately save time (and spare yourself a panic attack or crying session) by proactively prioritizing social time.

✳ Doing You

Take time each day to do something that rejuvenates your mind, body, or spirit (or all three!). Even 10 minutes of bird watching, reading, painting—or whatever else you enjoy—can settle your mind and boost your life satisfaction.

Don't try to copy another teacher's healthy habits by doing something that stresses you out! Experiment until you figure out what works for you. Tiffany sets aside 15–20 minutes to sit in her car when she gets home each day to decompress and gather her thoughts. "I'm an introvert, so teaching is draining. That's why I take time to enjoy some silence or my own company before getting on with my night."

THINK Which of these healthy habits are already part of your life? Which do you struggle with? How could you integrate them into your routines?

Connect & Reflect

Use this Healthy Habit Tracker to track one or two (or more—it's up to you!) healthy habits from the previous pages. You may want to choose one you do pretty consistently and one you'd like to adopt. As you track your performance over a week, jot down patterns you see emerging.

Then, reflect on the impact your habits have had on your overall well-being. Did you notice anything about how you felt and managed stress? What small shifts might you make in your daily routine to ensure healthy habits?

DOWNLOAD HERE!

☑ HEALTHY HABIT TRACKER

Month:

Habit: _____

My motivation:

_____

_____

_____

_____

S	M	T	W	T	F	S
☐	☐	☐	☐	☐	☐	☐
☐	☐	☐	☐	☐	☐	☐
☐	☐	☐	☐	☐	☐	☐
☐	☐	☐	☐	☐	☐	☐
☐	☐	☐	☐	☐	☐	☐

Habit: _____

My motivation:

_____

_____

_____

_____

S	M	T	W	T	F	S
☐	☐	☐	☐	☐	☐	☐
☐	☐	☐	☐	☐	☐	☐
☐	☐	☐	☐	☐	☐	☐
☐	☐	☐	☐	☐	☐	☐
☐	☐	☐	☐	☐	☐	☐

Habit: _____

My motivation:

_____

_____

_____

_____

S	M	T	W	T	F	S
☐	☐	☐	☐	☐	☐	☐
☐	☐	☐	☐	☐	☐	☐
☐	☐	☐	☐	☐	☐	☐
☐	☐	☐	☐	☐	☐	☐
☐	☐	☐	☐	☐	☐	☐

WHAT ABOUT ROUTINES THAT JUST AREN'T WORKING?

It's not a sign of failure if a routine isn't clicking for you and your students, despite repeated practice. But fixing it takes awareness and patience.

Take a minute to identify obstacles or sticking points. It might be time to make a change if you can answer "yes" to any of these questions.

QUESTION	YES	NO
Is the routine draining time or energy? Routines are supposed to simplify life. Feel free to discard or rework any routines that take too much time or energy.	☐	☐
Is the routine causing stress or confusion? Routines should bring clarity, not chaos. If things feel more complicated than before, it's a sign to adjust your routine.	☐	☐
Have circumstances changed since you established the routine? A change in school policy, like the addition of school breakfast or staggered dismissal times, might necessitate a change to morning or end-of-school-day routines. The addition of a new family member (or pet) at home will almost definitely require some adaptations to your morning and evening routines.	☐	☐
Are you or your students bored? Slogging through a stale routine isn't the answer. Keep things fresh by adding new elements. In the classroom, consider using new code words or clean-up songs. Looking for more inspiration for clean-up songs and other classroom routines to keep students engaged and excited?	☐	☐

"Don't assume every routine will work perfectly and don't wait until next year or after a school break to change it. Take action now—that will relieve your stress and help kids see that even our best laid plans are works in progress."

—**MORGAN MERCADO,**
third-grade teacher

TIPS FOR REVISING ROUTINES

* **Talk about why you're considering a change.** "Don't just change a routine without telling kids why," says Hannah Kittle, fifth-grade teacher. "You can be honest with them: This is what I've observed happening, and this is why this isn't working for our class. How can we make our routines better? What do you all think would be more successful?"

* **Involve your students.** Ask students what they like (and don't like) about your current routine. Ask them what's not working. Together, brainstorm new ideas. If students suggest something impractical or unsafe, thank them for their input and explain why the suggestion won't work.

* **Introduce the new routine.** Use the previously described tips and strategies, including the Gradual Release of Responsibility.

* **Practice.** It'll take time for students to adopt a new routine. Don't be surprised if a few of them occasionally revert to the "old way" of doing things. Simply redirect them and remind them of the new routine.

Hannah's fifth graders enjoy taking part in discussing what to change and how best to do it.

"Excellent teaching requires innovation, which means we have to look for ways to change our routines even if it's going to complicate things at first."

—**PAUL KING,** sixth-grade teacher

Simple, purposeful routines streamline necessary tasks, allowing you (and your students) more time for fun, creativity, and meaningful learning. Norms shape your classroom culture. Next, we'll explore how to create and apply class norms.

NORMS

NORMS 101

Classroom norms are shared expectations that help create a positive, effective learning environment. They provide guidelines for how everyone in the class should interact, work together, and manage their behavior. Some teachers prefer the term "agreements" to "norms."

Because norms provide clear behavioral expectations, they:

- ⭐ Help students feel safe and secure
- ⭐ Decrease misbehavior
- ⭐ Build student independence
- ⭐ Support the classroom community

Did you know...?
Giving students the opportunity to co-create class rules promotes school connectedness, which is linked to improved academic outcomes and student well-being (Wilkins et al., 2023).

"Investing the time into teaching your expectations can lead to deep conversations about how our behavior affects others."

—BREANN FENNELL, third-grade teacher

DRAFT A CLASS CONTRACT

You could walk into your room and post a list of class rules on Day 1. But you'll get more buy-in from your students—and better behavior —if you work together to create shared agreements. Here's how:

Step 1: Introduce the Idea

If you have early elementary students, consider a read-aloud to get them thinking about classroom expectations. (One to consider: *David Goes to School* by David Shannon.) Older elementary students may be familiar with the idea of class norms, and can share helpful insights about what works and what doesn't.

NOTE: Your school likely has building-wide norms that you can discuss and share with your students. Together, explore the "why" behind school and classroom norms (walking versus running in the halls, for instance, helps students stay safe).

Step 2: Brainstorm

Sixth-grade teacher Grace Hearl starts by asking her students, "What does a successful classroom look like for teacher and students?" If they're stuck, she'll ask the opposite question—"What does a NOT successful classroom look like?" That typically generates lots of responses!

Tim Wheeler, a third-grade teacher, asks his students to "brainstorm what we want people to say about our class." Then, he helps them think about what behaviors and actions might lead to those descriptors.

Write your students' ideas on the smartboard, whiteboard, or chart paper.

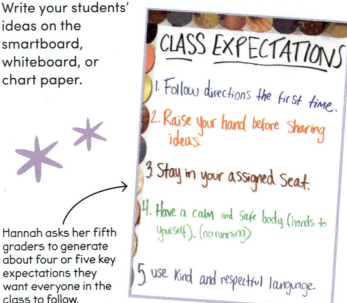

CLASS EXPECTATIONS

1. Follow directions the first time.
2. Raise your hand before sharing ideas.
3. Stay in your assigned seat.
4. Have a calm and safe body (hands to yourself). (no running)
5. Use kind and respectful language.

Hannah asks her fifth graders to generate about four or five key expectations they want everyone in the class to follow.

Step 3: Review, Consolidate, and Elaborate

Together, review the class's ideas. Look for themes and connections. You might want to use a graphic organizer to help students flesh out their thoughts.

Tim crafts students' ideas into a mission statement, and then workshops it with the kids. Together, they may decide to eliminate some ideas and elaborate on others. Some classes also personalize their contract with a title, such as *The Gibson Scholars Agreement*, or open with a preamble, such as *We, the members of Room 217, ...*

Tim's students start with an idea brainstorm about what qualities will make them great community members. They then select the most important qualities and, together, shape them into a two-sentence mission statement.

Did you know...?
Reinforcing prosocial behaviors and consistently enforcing shared agreements can promote equity in the classroom (Wilkins et al., 2023).

Step 4: Formalize Your Class Contract

Write up your shared agreements and have everyone in the class sign their name to indicate their commitment to upholding the contract.

Step 5: Post Your Contract

Hang your class contract in a highly visible area so that your norms remain top-of-mind. Refer to it often—especially when recognizing good behavior!

It's also important to send copies of your class contract to students' families, so that caregivers understand classroom expectations and can help reinforce them as needed. (Find tips and strategies for connecting and communicating with families in Part 3.)

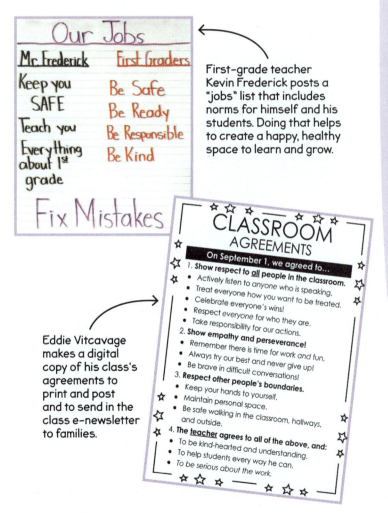

First-grade teacher Kevin Frederick posts a "jobs" list that includes norms for himself and his students. Doing that helps to create a happy, healthy space to learn and grow.

Eddie Vitcavage makes a digital copy of his class's agreements to print and post and to send in the class e-newsletter to families.

YOUR EXPECTATIONS MATTER, TOO

As the teacher, it's up to you to ensure that your classroom is a safe, functional space. So, while it's important to involve students in establishing norms, it's okay for you to insist on nonnegotiables.

"I preface my expectations by telling my class, 'In order to be an effective teacher for everyone, I need everyone to follow these expectations,'" Grace Hearl says. "I also give the reason behind my expectations and explain that I will hold students to them."

Connect & Reflect

Follow these steps to think through how you'll establish and maintain norms in your classroom.

DOWNLOAD HERE!

 CREATE A CLASS CONTRACT!

STEP 1: Introduce the idea. Think: How can you make the idea engaging and understandable?	Strategies I'll use to introduce the idea:
STEP 2: Brainstorm. Think: How will you record students' ideas?	Questions I'll ask to encourage students to generate ideas:
STEP 3: Review, consolidate, and elaborate. Think: How can you show the value of restating and revising as you lead the activity?	Tools I'll use to organize and help students refine their thoughts:
STEPS 4 & 5: Formalize and post. Think: How will you let families know about the contract the class created and how it can become a resource for you in your home-school communication?	Ways I'll keep the contract visible and in use to reinforce positive behavior:

CLASSROOM ENGAGEMENT

Classroom norms should guide students' behaviors and actions. But students need support and practice as they learn to apply norms in a variety of situations.

Students will daydream, get distracted, and attempt to distract others—because they're human.

No one—not even adults!—can stay on task all the time. Giving students tools to help them manage flagging attention can help them apply class norms, such as "respect others," "stay on task," and "be responsible."

Did you know...?
We're often told that a child's attention span ranges from 2 to 3 minutes per year of age. But you might find that's generous! One recent study showed that 7 minutes was the longest first graders could demonstrate on-task behavior (Asprilia et al., 2020).

Classroom Engagement Spectrum

Grace Hearl uses a classroom engagement spectrum (Fisher et al., 2020, adapted by Meghan Hargrave) to communicate expectations and empower students. The spectrum visually represents various levels of engagement using a positive and negative number scale: –3, –2, –1, 0, 1, 2, 3, with –3 indicating completely off-task behavior and 3 denoting fully learner-driven behavior. Strong verbs like "disrupt" and "drive" are paired with actions students can relate to, like "making it hard for others" and "leading others." (If you have younger students, you could use a 0–6 number scale or pictures instead.)

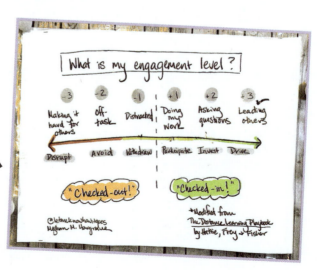

Hargrave's engagement spectrum poster serves as a quick reference to help Grace's students gauge the degree to which they're "checked in" or "checked out." Students also have smaller versions at their desks.

Together, Grace and her class discuss the fact that attention is affected by numerous factors and can change. They talk about engagement expectations for various tasks, including teacher-led lessons and group work. And then, they brainstorm strategies they can use to boost engagement when needed, such as moving to another area (if the student is finding it difficult to focus in place).

"I tell them, 'I'm not asking you to be at a 3 all the time. That would exhaust us. I'm not even asking you to not be at –1. But let's talk about what we can do when we're low,'" Grace says.

Grace uses those class-generated suggestions to create an anchor chart of engagement-boosting strategies, which she posts in the classroom. The Classroom Engagement Spectrum is also posted (see previous page)—and each student has a mini-version attached to their desk. During class, Grace can simply flash a number on her fingers or point to the spectrum on a student's desk to indicate that it's time for a change.

BreAnn Fennell teaches a tried-and-true group playgound game, and then asks students to record and post the rules for reference. That's procedural writing practice with a purpose!

MATERIAL MANAGEMENT

Crayons. Scissors. Laptops.

Many of your students likely know how to use these common tools, but you may need to teach them how to apply norms, such as "be safe" and "be responsible," as they use learning materials in the classroom. Establishing expectations for materials now will save you time and frustration later. Here's how:

* **Introduce the material and share your expectations.** Say something like "We're going to use laptops today. While I pass them out, please put your hands either on your shoulders or on your knees, whichever is comfortable."

* **Support exploration.** "When you give a student a material they've never seen before and tell them not to play with it, they're going to play with it," says Kevin Frederick, first-grade teacher. Instead of getting frustrated, build in (limited!) time for exploration.

* **Empower students to solve potential problems.** Tell them what to do when common problems occur. What do you want them to do if their laptop loses charge?

* **Describe what you want students to do with the tool.** Keep it simple.

* **Monitor. Provide positive reinforcement.** Verbal and visual reinforcement of expectations can keep students on track.

* **Share end-of-activity expectations.** Say something like, "We've got one more minute. When I say [code word], close your laptop."

* **Review and reinforce.** Together, discuss what went well and what could have gone better. Reiterate your material management expectations. Consider creating and posting anchor charts near frequently used items to help students remember these expectations.

Did you know...? Students report feeling more connected to their peers when teachers actively take steps to promote positive interactions and friendships (Wilkins et al., 2023).

Michele Ogden's second and third graders return their device to the laptop cart by dropping it off in the slot with their assigned number.

NORMS

You can't *make* students follow your classroom norms. Your role is to model norms and support students when they struggle to follow them.

MANAGE YOUR EMOTIONS

Pay attention to *your* reaction when students violate shared agreements. Although it's normal to feel disappointed or frustrated, remember: Kids do well if they *can* (Greene, 2010). Their behavior isn't a direct reflection of your effectiveness as a teacher; their behavior indicates a need for additional support. If you feel your heart racing and temperature rising, take a few deep breaths. Pause. Calm yourself. Always manage your emotions before responding to student behavior.

The Chill Checklist
WHEN YOU READ THIS: DRINK WATER!!

With Students
- Circulate in the classroom; take time to check in with students.
- Take a quick look out the window while monitoring.
- Use a breathing strategy.
- Grab a quick snack/treat.
- Open the windows to let in fresh air.

Whole-Class Resets
- Mindful Moments on YouTube (Meditations, Calming Videos)
- Change up the lighting.
- Movement Breaks to release extra energy or to excite students
- Brief whole-class meeting to check in
- Class read-aloud (can target specific SEL skills)
- Play quiet background music.

Watch this!

Eddie Vitcavage's Chill Checklist gives him quick reminders to stay calm and collected. He explains how he uses it in this video.

"Allow yourself to be frustrated, to be upset. We name feelings in my class, so I openly share my feelings with my kids and model self-regulation techniques. I'll say, 'I'm taking a big belly breath right now because I'm feeling frustrated.'"

—KEVIN FREDERICK, first-grade teacher

BE A COACH

Adopt a Ted Lasso-like approach to classroom management. Be positive, empathetic, and confident in your students' potential. Don't default to punishment. Instead, calmly review the situation and behavior, as a coach does when players miss a critical play. Address any misunderstandings or miscommunication. Provide additional coaching and skills development, as needed.

Harness student power. If one student's behavior is negatively affecting the whole classroom, it's likely that student is a social powerhouse. Privately point out how their behavior is affecting the class—and what they might do instead to become a positive leader.

Use positive reinforcement. Reinforcing positive behavior is almost always more effective than calling out negative behavior. And positive reinforcement has additional benefits, including:

⭐ Increased student engagement
⭐ Improved student confidence
⭐ Increased student motivation
⭐ Positive classroom environment

Positive reinforcement is related to increased attendance because kids who enjoy school are more likely to go to school on a regular basis (Craig, 2019; Williams, 2021).

This small pocket chart displays stickers students can purchase when their ROAR card is drawn. (See Michele Ogden's ROAR incentive system, page 27.)

Did you know...? Studies show that positive reinforcement of desired behavior increases student time on-task (Caldarella et al., 2020).

"If your classroom management problems are coming from one student, they usually have a lot of power in the classroom. So, empower them in a positive way."

—GRACE HEARL,
sixth-grade teacher

Group Punishment Is Never a Good Idea

Our students will tell us this any time we try it—and they are always right: Group punishment *isn't* fair. Withholding a privilege (or inflicting a consequence) on an entire class due to the behavior of a few is more likely to stoke resentment and anger than it is to trigger positive behavior. Group punishment can also lead to peer bullying and classroom division instead of class cohesion (Thomas, 2019).

"Group punishment is something I look back on and regret. There is no benefit to group punishment."

—GRACE HEARL, sixth-grade teacher

Did you experience group punishment as a child? How did you feel about it? Did the punishment positively affect the behavior of the class? What do you think a more effective response might have been?

REINFORCE & REMIND

Students need regular reminders of class norms. It's a good idea to review your class contract:

* On Monday mornings early in the school year, as students are learning your expectations

* After long holiday breaks

* When a new student joins the class

* Approximately once a month, especially for the first quarter or semester

* Whenever students are struggling to meet expectations

REMEMBER: You can add to or revise your class contract as needed. Tim Wheeler and his class revise their mission statement two or three times a year (see page 36). It's a great opportunity to show the revision of an important document—for a real purpose—in action!

ROUTINES & NORMS SEND-OFF

If you reached this page, you've absorbed lots of tips and tools!

Big Ideas to Keep in Mind

✳ When you develop consistent routines and norms, you create a strong foundation for a positive learning environment—and for student independence.

✳ Your routines should make daily tasks more manageable for you and your students. But they don't have to be boring or in lockstep—you and your students can design them to fit your preferences, personalities, and class culture.

✳ Developing self-care routines will reduce your stress and boost your ability to manage your day.

✳ Inviting your students to help create class norms gives them a powerful sense of ownership, and makes them more likely to follow the norms.

✳ Using praise and positive reinforcement encourages desired behaviors.

✳ Give yourself and your students grace. Learning takes effort and time. Celebrate evidence of progress, no matter how small, as you discover how to work, share space and materials, and be in community together.

INSTEAD OF THINKING "Are we there yet?" **THINK** "How did we make progress today?"

Tim Wheeler leaves us with two lines from a mission statement his class co-created: "We will work hard through our struggles to grow. We will laugh and celebrate as we achieve our goals."

Here's a quote you can display to spark discussion with students about their learning.

PART 2
TIME & SPACE

ORGANIZING DAILY CLASSROOM LIFE

Hannah Kittle's first classroom was not a blank space. "The closets were stuffed with the most random stuff—decades old, covered in dust," she recalls. Unsure of what to do with the leftover materials, Hannah did what most new teachers do: She left them alone and worked around them.

Eventually, Hannah realized that she needed to take charge of her time and space. Working around accumulated clutter was both time-consuming and energy-draining. Hannah ditched the outdated materials and added personal touches.

Like Hannah, you probably didn't get to choose your classroom—or your schedule. Learning how to most efficiently use your available time and space can power up your classroom management.

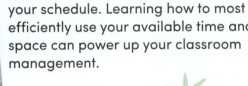

Consolidating and organizing her materials enabled Hannah to create a quiet reading corner in the back of her classroom that helps her fifth graders calm down and focus.

LET'S BEGIN

Think of time and space as raw materials you can use to construct your learning environment. The sections ahead will help you take stock of your scheduled and unscheduled time, as well as your classroom space. Then they will help you apply veteran-teacher tips and tools to manage that time and space.

But before you dive in, take a moment to consider your goals and preferences and your students' needs:

⭐ What activities will occur regularly in your classroom?

⭐ What do you want your classroom vibe to be?

⭐ How do you want to feel in your space? What do you hope your students feel?

⭐ How do you expect students to interact within the space?

In this section, you'll learn:

✳ How to create a workable schedule

✳ Techniques to maximize learning time

✳ Strategies to reduce your workload

✳ How to set up a classroom that promotes student autonomy

✳ Ways to organize materials and resources for easy access

✳ How to maintain a welcoming learning environment

> **RULE OF THUMB:** Time and space are finite resources. Your time does not expand to meet demands and neither does your classroom space. Accepting and working within the limitations of time and space will help you to prioritize effectively and protect your well-being.

Kevin Frederick organizes an interactive space for calendar math, where students participate in counting, tallying, graphing, and developing time and calendar concepts every day.

TIME

TIME MANAGEMENT 101

Well-used time is one of your most valuable resources.

Efficient use of teacher time:

* Increases productivity
* Decreases stress
* Prevents burnout

Efficient use of class time:

* Increases student engagement
* Decreases misbehavior
* Supports student learning

Eddie Vitcavage's daily schedule is easy for his fifth graders to scan. In seconds, he can adjust and print or display it.

"There are so many demands outside of the classroom that I didn't expect, like meetings and paperwork. Who knew the majority of my time after school would be spent filling out behavior charts for school counselors, attending faculty meetings, and submitting grades?"

—**HANNAH KITTLE,** fifth-grade teacher

GET THE BIG PICTURE

You have a lot of responsibilities besides teaching students. There are meetings, recess duty, professional-development sessions, administrative responsibilities, and family outreach. Learning to prioritize and allocate your time can decrease stress.

Your to-do list may feel overwhelming—because teachers are asked to do a lot! Thoughtfully structuring your time can help you feel more in control. Start by drafting a list of your obligations, and then devise a plan to manage them.

To develop a workable plan, you'll also need a realistic understanding of your available time and energy. Ignoring the very real limitations of time and energy will leave you prone to burnout; carefully prioritizing tasks and protecting your time ensures you're more successful and satisfied.

If your list of responsibilities seems disproportionate to your available time and energy, breathe! You can take steps, starting with the following tips and tools, to make your workload more manageable.

"Lesson planning takes a big chunk of your time: Knowing what you're teaching, how you're teaching it, and why it matters will help you put a thoughtful plan in place—and save time."

—PAUL KING,
sixth-grade teacher

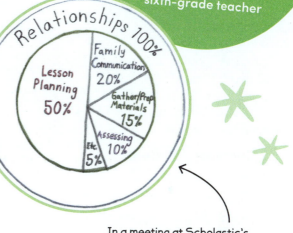

In a meeting at Scholastic's New York headquarters, a team of Teacher Fellows drew this chart to show the approximate time they spend on the five non-instructional responsibilities they find most time-consuming. They then drew a second outer circle to show how they consider relationship-building to be front and center in all they do.

 **THINK** What are your nonteaching obligations? Don't forget grading, lesson planning and preparation, family communication, school committees, and required meetings.

HERE'S HOW

1 **Determine your priorities.** What tasks are most important? Your answer to this question will depend on your values and job requirements. If "connecting with families" is among your top values, you'll want to make sure to allot time for phone calls or visits, while maintaining time for essential tasks like grading.

2 **Set boundaries.** Decide when you will begin and end your workday. Then communicate your availability to students, families, and colleagues—and stick to it.

3 **Delegate.**
What are you doing that students could do for themselves? Consider tasks, such as classroom cleanup, restocking materials, or handing out papers. Are there any tasks you could delegate to interested family members or school volunteers?

4 **Collaborate.** You don't have to do everything yourself. Your colleagues may be willing to share lesson plans, materials, and activity ideas.

Tap into the expertise of building specialists, too! Speech-language pathologists, reading specialists, and ELL teachers can provide invaluable assistance.

Morgan Mercado's team plans each week on a slide, creating a slideshow for each nine-week period. They link everything to this slideshow (daily plans, tests, etc.). This "hub" allows administrators, staff, and interns access to each teacher's plans for walk-throughs, observations, and class coverage, so everyone can know what to expect!

"The first year I was teaching, I would be up all times of night, replying to messages from parents. Now, I set boundaries up front. Parents know they can reach me between the hours of 7:00 am and 4:30 pm."

—TIFFANY YOUNG-NORRIS, kindergarten teacher

Michele Ogden puts classroom and school requests for parent volunteers at the top of her weekly newsletter.

Connect & Reflect

Try this exercise once your school year is underway.

DOWNLOAD HERE!

 MANAGING YOUR WORKLOAD

1 **List the key tasks that make up your current workload.** Include all responsibilities and activities that don't involve students, such as lesson planning, administrative tasks, grading, contacting parents, extracurricular activities, assigned supervision time, meetings, and volunteer activities. Estimate how much time you spend on each task each day. (You may need to take the average time for certain tasks across the week.)

2 **Get a clear picture of your time by creating a pie chart.** Use your task list and time estimates to represent your current situation, like the one on page 49. You may want to focus on a subset of your responsibilities that feels overly time-consuming, such as school-related responsibilities beyond instruction.

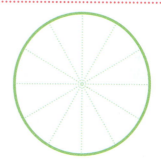

3 **Brainstorm ways to reduce your workload by 10–20%.** CONSIDER: Are you spending most of your time on the most important tasks? Can you eliminate, delegate, or collaborate on any tasks?

TIP: Use mentor meetings to your advantage: "You can ask for help with ways to save time on tasks like grading," advises Hannah Kittle.

4 **Pick one or two tasks to target.** Identify one or two time-saving strategies for each task.

To reduce my workload, I am going to…

5 **Reevaluate your workload in two weeks.** Have you managed to decrease the time you spent on certain tasks? Can you eliminate or delegate any additional tasks? It may be helpful to determine your top priority for the next week and concentrate your effort (and time) toward tasks that help you achieve that goal, while giving minimal time and effort to any other necessary tasks.

If you're stuck and don't see a way forward, ask a more experienced teacher for input. Record your progress by making a second, reorganized priority list or a new pie chart.

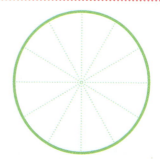

Revisit this exercise whenever you feel overwhelmed.

CREATING A WORKABLE SCHEDULE

Whether you like to plan in detail or just set a few primary goals for each part of the day, here are some things to keep in mind.

* **Be flexible.** Unplanned disruptions—such as student nosebleeds and fire alarm malfunctions—are all too common in classrooms. Build flexibility into your plans and adapt as needed.

* **Almost everything takes longer than you think it will.** Don't underestimate the amount of time needed for routine tasks. Instead, plan extra time for each task—and if you finish early, use the extra time to tackle another task on your to-do list.

* **Perfection isn't necessary.** A "good enough" lesson plan will get the job done—remember that you can improve it with reflection and practice. The extra half hour or hour (or longer!) you spend perfecting a good lesson plan may be better spent on rest or relaxation.

  If you struggle with perfection, try allotting yourself a reasonable amount of time for a task, such as grading student work. (Not sure how long it should take? Ask a colleague.) Set a timer. Try to complete the task before the timer dings.

Your time management skills will improve with experience. Be patient with yourself!

"I've learned to grade at least two assignments each week and input them into the system, so that when grades are due, I'm not panicking."

—**HANNAH KITTLE**, fifth-grade teacher

KEEP 'EM ON TASK

Keeping students engaged during lessons will minimize distractions and disruptions—and help you efficiently teach the required material. Try these strategies:

Embrace Student Interests

Kids pay attention when you're talking about things that matter to them. So weave student interests into your lessons. If you've got sports fans in your class, create math problems that involve their favorite teams; have them calculate the total number of points scored in a game or figure out how many more points Team A needs to beat Team B. Read books that feature their favorite characters, and help connect content to student interests. Be mindful of your students' diverse cultural backgrounds, and invite families to share stories and traditions that reflect their experiences and heritage.

Plan Short Lessons

Break up class time into multiple short lessons. Student attention wanes during lengthy, whole-group lessons—and that's when kids start fidgeting and messing around with their neighbors. The longer the lesson, the more off-task behavior. Several 10-minute lessons on a topic are almost always more effective than fewer 30-minute lessons (Godwin et al., 2016).

SPOTLIGHT ON MANAGING TIME

"Purposeful, intentional engagement is a big part of classroom management. If you don't know what you want your students to be doing at a certain time, how will they?"

—GRACE HEARL,
sixth-grade teacher

Check Out These Books!

Revolutionary Love series

You'll find practices to use throughout the day that affirm and celebrate all students' identities, languages, and cultures—building a community of engaged, valued, and compassionate learners.

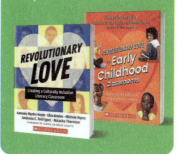

Rotate Stations

Having groups of students rotate through various learning activities (which can be set up in different areas of your room) addresses students' need for movement and variety. Hands-on activities, collaborative discussions, and digital experiences encourage active participation and help break longer class periods into more manageable, focused segments. This structure empowers students to take ownership of their learning, promotes social interaction, and can even support differentiated instruction by offering various levels of challenge at each station.

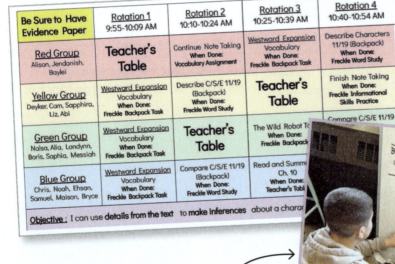

Be Sure to Have Evidence Paper	Rotation 1 9:55-10:09 AM	Rotation 2 10:10-10:24 AM	Rotation 3 10:25-10:39 AM	Rotation 4 10:40-10:54 AM
Red Group Alison, Jendanish, Baylei	**Teacher's Table**	Continue Note Taking When Done: Vocabulary Assignment	Westward Expansion Vocabulary When Done: Freckle Backpack Task	Describe Characters 11/19 (Backpack) When Done: Freckle Word Study
Yellow Group Deyker, Cam, Sapphira, Liz, Abi	Westward Expansion Vocabulary When Done: Freckle Backpack Task	Describe C/S/E 11/19 (Backpack) When Done: Freckle Word Study	**Teacher's Table**	Finish Note Taking When Done: Freckle Informational Skills Practice
Green Group Nalsa, Alia, Londynn, Boris, Sophia, Messiah	Westward Expansion Vocabulary When Done: Freckle Backpack Task	**Teacher's Table**	The Wild Robot Today When Done: Freckle Backpack	Compare C/S/E 11/19
Blue Group Chris, Noah, Ehsan, Samuel, Maison, Bryce	Westward Expansion Vocabulary When Done: Freckle Backpack Task	Compare C/S/E 11/19 (Backpack) When Done: Freckle Word Study	Read and Summe Ch. 10 When Done: Teacher's Table	

Objective : I can use **details from the text** to make **inferences** about a charac

Eddie Vitcavage's fifth graders rotate stations as they work on both independent and group-based comprehension tasks. Eddie meets with small, need-based groups during the Teacher's Table rotation.

Maintain Students' Motivation and Energy

When it's time for small-group work, teacher Grace Hearl posts a countdown timer on the smartboard, so students can see at a glance how much time is left before groups switch. Individual timers are particularly helpful for children with attention challenges because they can be used discreetly and help students pace their efforts.

Consider these ideas for using music and lighting as nonverbal signals and energy moderators:

⭐ Put on upbeat music when students are brainstorming. (Most pop songs last about three to four minutes, so you have a built-in time limit.)

⭐ Play calming music and dim the lights when it's time to settle down.

⭐ Use color-changing string lights to encourage acceptable movement and noise levels.

BREAK TIME!

Human brains need breaks to learn effectively. Physical activity increases the flow of blood and oxygen to the brain, which enhances neural connections and memory. Mental breaks help us learn because our brains "practice" and consolidate skills during rest (Buch et al., 2021).

Students (and teachers!) benefit from two key types of breaks.

① Movement moments

Opportunities to get up, stretch, and release energy Intersperse breaks throughout the day, especially after periods of intense concentration (or lots of sitting!).

Try "Dolphin Dive" and three other energizing breaks when energy is dragging!

Try "3-D Breathing" and three other calming activities to get kids refocused.

② Calming intervals

Times to relax, reset, and refocus for the next activity Calming intervals are helpful after high-energy activities, including class celebrations and conflicts.

Spontaneous breaks can also be super effective. When fifth-grade teacher Eddie Vitcavage notices a lot of pencil tapping and "fidgety legs," he adds movement to his lesson (perhaps by posing multiple-choice questions and having students go to the corner of the room associated with their chosen answer) or announces a one-minute stretch.

DOWNLOAD HERE!

STREAMLINE PLANNING

Before devoting a lot of time to lesson planning, get the lay of the land: Does your school or district use a specific curriculum and require structured pacing? If so, lessons may be mapped out for you. Touch base with your mentor, instructional coach, and teammates to find out what areas you'll need to plan and what requirements or standards to use as your guide.

You may want to borrow lesson plans and materials from your fellow teachers, who can also help you figure out ways to differentiate those materials to meet the needs of all students. Use ready-to-go online resources, such as Scholastic Teachables, to further streamline class planning.

"Make sure you don't over-commit yourself. Some of our new teachers are in the building until 9 PM. Give yourself a hard break by saying, 'I'm going to work on this for an hour max'—and then go home.'"

—MELANIE OKADIGWE, Pre-K–sixth grade learning specialist

It can be helpful to start out with a simple, no-frills template to organize your ideas and schedule your time.

DOWNLOAD HERE!

As you incorporate more scheduling requirements, you may find it helpful to design your own version, as Eddie Vitcavage does in his Master Schedule spreadsheet.

Weekly Schedule

Year at a Glance

August | September | October | November

Curriculum Plans & Goals

Reading | Writing | Math

February | March
June | July

Grade 5 2024-25 Master Schedule

Monday		Tuesday		Wednesday		Thursday		Friday	
8:45-9:05	Arrival/Breakfast	8:45-9:05	Arrival/Breakfast	8:45-9:05	Arrival/Breakfast	8:45-9:05	Arrival/Breakfast	8:45-9:05	Arrival/Breakfast
9:05-9:25	SEL	9:05-9:25	SEL	9:05-9:25	SEL	9:05-9:25	SEL	9:05-9:25	SEL
9:25-10:20	ELA/Reading Rotations	9:25-10:55	ELA/Reading Rotations	9:25-10:55	ELA/Reading Rotations	9:25-10:55	Math/Math Rotations	9:25-10:55	ELA/Reading Rotations
10:21-11:00	Music/Prep	11:00-11:20	Recess	11:00-11:20	Recess	11:00-11:20	Recess	11:00-11:20	Recess
11:01-11:20	Recess	11:20-11:50	Lunch	11:20-11:50	Lunch	11:20-11:50	Lunch	11:20-11:50	Lunch
11:20-11:50	Lunch	11:55-1:25	Math/Math Rotations	11:55-1:25	Math/Math Rotations	11:55-12:50	Reading Rotations	11:55-1:25	Math/Math Rotations
11:55-12:55	Reading Rotations	1:30-1:45	Flex Time	1:30-1:45	Flex Time	12:50-1:45	Science	1:27-2:10	Science/Writing
12:55-2:25	Math/Math Rotations	1:46-2:26	Physical Education/Prep	1:46-2:26	Art/Prep	1:46-2:26	Technology/Prep	2:10-2:25	Flex Time/Prize Box
2:30-3:15	Social Studies	2:30-3:15	Writing	2:30-2:45	Writing	2:30-2:45	Flex Time	2:26-3:09	Enrichment/Prep
3:15-3:20	Pack Up	3:15-3:20	Pack Up	2:45-2:50	Pack Up	2:45-2:50	Pack Up	3:10-3:15	Flex Time/Pack Up
3:20-3:35	Dismissal	3:20-3:35	Dismissal	2:50-3:05	Dismissal	2:50-3:05	Dismissal	3:20-3:35	Dismissal

9:50-10:15	AM Bathroom Time
1:00-1:15	Monday PM Bathroom

Prep Periods

Rest and recharge, or hunker down and get some work done? You can do either (or both) during your prep period.

Devoting your student-free time to grading and lesson planning can minimize (or eliminate) the amount of work you take home. Taking time to relax during your prep period can be a sanity saver, but it might also mean having to tackle a few tasks after hours. You get to decide which approach makes the most sense for you on any given day.

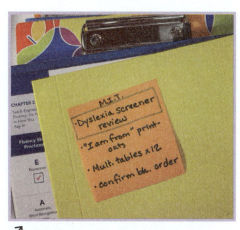

Melanie Okadigwe devotes the first 15 minutes of her prep periods to whatever is her most important task (MIT) for the day. That helps her avoid distraction and ensure that she doesn't "get so far behind," she says.

Time Management Tools

Experienced teachers swear by:

* **Calendars.** It doesn't matter if you use a paper or digital calendar. Pick a calendar tool that works for you and use it to track your daily obligations, important dates, and upcoming tasks. Set "due dates" for yourself as needed to ensure that essential tasks (like grade entry) are completed in a timely fashion.

* **Timers.** Whether you're using it to help you focus on and finish that dreaded task or to remind you to take a break, check out a range of fun countdown timers on YouTube (students find these motivating, too!), as well as apps like BreakTimer that remind you to get up and stretch, breathe, or drink water.

In addition to her daily lesson plans, Hannah Kittle uses a big desk calendar for sketching out weekly and monthly tasks and reminders.

Connect & Reflect

Use your preferred calendar to organize an upcoming week. Consider using different colors or symbols for each step below to see the areas you focus on across the day and week.

DOWNLOAD HERE!

 ## WEEKLY TIME MANAGEMENT

STEP 1 **Schedule your school obligations.**	Enter all your school commitments for the week: • Instructional time • Meetings (staff, parent-teacher conferences) • Duties (recess, lunch) • Other scheduled school events
STEP 2 **Add out-of-school commitments.**	Now, include your personal obligations: • Family commitments • Personal appointments • Social events or errands
STEP 3 **Schedule time for essential teaching tasks.**	Slot in time for the essential tasks that you might otherwise put off: • **Grading:** Choose specific days/times for grading assignments. Aim for smaller, manageable blocks rather than long sessions. • **Lesson planning:** Pick a time to prepare next week's lessons. • **Family communication:** Dedicate a short, focused time daily or every other day to handle communications.
STEP 4 **Don't forget self-care!**	Carve out time for exercise, hobbies, or simply relaxing. **TIP:** *Do not skip self-care.* (See pages 25–27 for mood- and health-boosting tips!)
STEP 5 **Review and adjust.**	Are there any tasks you can delegate or skip? **TIP:** First-grade teacher Kevin Frederick recommends setting aside a regular time to do weekly planning. Which day and time works best for you?

Weekly Schedule

Time	Monday	Tuesday	Wednesday	Thursday	Friday

See page 56 for a weekly schedule to download.

DEALING WITH DISTRACTIONS

Class time won't always go as planned. In fact, it's best to expect (and plan for) disruptions. Teachers frequently experience two types of distractions:

1 **Spontaneous surprises,** including emergencies, accidents, and "pop-in" visits from administrators or colleagues

2 **Student concerns,** which may include off-topic questions, curiosity-driven interruptions, and behaviors such as restlessness or side conversations

Here's how to manage them:

✯ **Stay calm.** When you're faced with a spontaneous surprise or a student concern, take deep breaths as needed to maintain your composure. Emotions can be contagious, so if you lose your cool, your students probably will as well.

✯ **Prioritize safety.** Your students' well-being is your number one concern. If a student is experiencing a medical issue, address it immediately and seek help if needed. In the event of an external danger, such as a fire or unsafe behavior, move your students to safety and follow established emergency protocols.

"If I have to deal with an urgent interruption, I ask students to do tasks they can handle completely independently. For example, they can play low-prep reinforcement games like 'Word Match' or use the listening center."

—BRIDGET JORDAN,
ESOL teacher

Equipping students to independently handle minor issues—like scraped knees and paper cuts—can save you time. Stock supplies in an easily accessible place and teach students how to use them.

 **THINK** What activities can you have on hand for students to do during disruptions?

⭐ **Acknowledge curiosity-driven interruptions.** An off-topic question can be a window into a student's mind. Thank students for their questions and curiosity and let them know when (and how) you will address their concerns.

⭐ **Ignore distractions that aren't negatively affecting the class.** Calling attention to behaviors like talking or doodling can amplify the disruption. It's better to continue class and, if possible, address the disruptive individual privately, at another time.

⭐ **Keep students on task.** When your attention is needed elsewhere, it's smart to have a handful of activities available to keep the rest of your class engaged. Plan ahead: Think of 3–5 activities students can do independently and keep the necessary materials stocked. (Good ideas include independent reading or drawing, puzzle sheets, and educational games connected to skills or content they're learning.) Introduce and practice these activities so students are ready to go when the moment arises.

"I was reading aloud a story about the civil rights movement when a student raised his hand and asked me 'How can I as a student be an activist?' That question opened my eyes to the fact that students want to talk about things connected to the curriculum. I told the student that this was a wonderful topic for us to discuss as a class and we made a plan to do just that at our next day's morning meeting."

—VALENTE' GIBSON, afterschool coordinator

One favorite activity students can learn to do on their own or in partners are word ladders, which have a repeatable format that incorporates phonics, decoding, and meaning-making. These pages from *Daily Word Ladders: Content Areas* (Grades 2–3 and 4–6) show you how to solve a word ladder—and how to make your own!

MAKE TIME FOR FUN

As busy as your days are, it's important to have fun! Yes, you have a lot of academic and administrative responsibilities, and you need to cover a lot of material. But strict adherence to pre-planned lessons and pacing guides can be counterproductive. Students learn best—and teachers thrive—when classes take time to play and laugh together.

Carpe Diem . . . With Purpose!

Our brains respond to novelty, encoding new memories that delight or pique our interest— Use this to your advantage when possible to boost students' engagement. Second-grade teacher Keke Powell dresses up to match a new unit theme, capturing student interest as they walk through the door.

When third-grade teacher Tim Wheeler donned a wig and adopted a humorously strict persona, his class "did a 45-minute lesson in 20 minutes," he said. Tim has since amassed a collection of wigs and added other characters to his repertoire, including "Mr. Hair," which he describes as an "aging British rock-star-type guy."

Of course, time management is just one aspect of classroom management. How you arrange and use the physical space in your classroom can also make a big impact. Up next, we'll dive into strategies for managing classroom space to support flexible and engaging learning experiences.

Watch Tim share his best time-saving tips, from flipped lessons to managing bathroom breaks!

Watch this!

SPACE

SPACE MANAGEMENT 101

Your ideal learning space may look different from your teammate's, but a few design principles hold true for any classroom: Crowded, cluttered spaces are difficult to navigate; welcoming, functional spaces allow room for creativity and collaboration.

Crowded, cluttered classrooms:

* Delay access to materials
* Contribute to misplacement of student work
* Add stress for students and teachers

Welcoming, functional classrooms:

* Promote a sense of well-being and belonging
* Ensure easy access to materials
* Reflect instructional goals
* Provide a range of spaces for different types of teaching and learning

Did you know...?
A study of 153 classrooms in 27 schools found that seven key design parameters—light, temperature, air quality, ownership, flexibility, complexity, and color—account for 16% of the variation in students' academic progress (Barrett et al., 2015).

"I don't want students walking into my classroom thinking, 'Oh, this is Mr. Frederick's house and we're just visiting.' I try to make it our space."

—**KEVIN FREDERICK,** first-grade teacher

What follows are three key design elements that researchers (and experienced classroom teachers) find have a powerful impact.

1 Naturalness

Humans tend to feel and perform better when they can see or experience nature. Students in classrooms with "more natural window views" report less stress and spend more time on task than students in windowless rooms (Lindemann-Matthies et al., 2021). (No windows? Bring nature inside. Think plants, natural materials, and nature-inspired décor. Stick to allergy-friendly plants, like succulents, golden pothos, and snake plants; steer clear of flowering or sporing plants, like ferns.)

Adding plants to his classroom spaces has really enhanced Eddie Vitcavage's self-care. He says, "I get to watch them grow, and the students become involved. Plus, plants purify the air, so it's win-win!"

2 Individualization

Kids do best in spaces that consider and reflect their needs and interests. Appropriately sized furniture, a choice of seating options, and décor that celebrates students can enhance their comfort and sense of belonging.

3 Stimulation

Aim for just the right amount of sensory stimulation. Lots of colors, posters, or educational charts can be overwhelming; bare walls are uninspiring. Light-colored walls combined with a feature wall and pops of color have "the best correlation with learning progress" (Barrett et al., 2015).

Sherri Amos's Reading Corner includes all these elements: a plant and natural light, a variety of seating options for students during read-alouds, an easy-to-browse library, and simple decor, including featured books on hanging wall shelves.

IDENTIFY & DEFINE YOUR GOALS

To set up and use your space most effectively, first identify and define your goals.

Learning Objectives

What tools and resources do students need to accomplish their learning goals? How can you utilize your shared space to accommodate their learning needs? In most classrooms, you'll want to create zones for various activities—a reading nook, for instance, to support and encourage reading; a "calm corner," or space students can utilize to manage emotions without disrupting the rest of the class; and a gathering area for group discussions.

Each of the books in Michele Ogden's bookshelf has a numbered sticker that coordinates with its basket for easy returns. Books are grouped into baskets based on text complexity, interests, and series/author sets.

"When it comes to classroom setup, keeping it flexible is super important for differentiation."

—EDDIE VITCAVAGE, fifth-grade teacher

Student Needs

How will you accommodate students' physical, emotional, and sensory needs? It's likely that your class includes students with a variety of learning preferences and neurodiverse traits. Some students may have ADHD, autism, sensory processing disorders, or difficulty with attachment, all of which can affect how they engage in the classroom. Some will benefit from distraction-free spaces, while others may need to move around to maintain focus. Offering flexible seating options in various sizes and configurations can help meet these diverse needs.

Technology

Where are the electrical outlets and power supplies located? How often will students be using technology? Do you need space for digital collaboration? You may also want to create a tech-free zone.

Accessibility

All students should be able to participate in instruction, so make sure furniture is sturdy and spaced in such a way that students with mobility challenges can safely maneuver. Whenever possible, share information in a variety of ways. Some students do best with pictorial messages; others prefer written words or audio. Think about how students with various physical, cognitive, and social needs may experience your classroom.

"A lot of my decisions about classroom organization are based on how I can help students to know what's going to happen next. I want to give them the capacity to do things for themselves."

—**KEVIN FREDERICK,**
first-grade teacher

Morgan Mercado keeps materials for indoor recess, like book sets, special mats, and board games, neatly organized on open shelves with ample spacing. This supports both accessibility and a sense of order and stability for students who experience sensory overload.

Morgan's organization system (on the right) includes clear labels on easy-to-reach drawers, different colors for turn-in baskets, and individual student work cubbies.

Watch this!

In this classroom tour, Kevin focuses on ways to make materials and experiences accessible to his first graders.

Connect & Reflect

Don't draw up any design plans just yet! Before you move any furniture or rethink displays, take time to assess your space and consider how it could best support learning.

DOWNLOAD HERE!

 SET THE STAGE

STEP 1 **Take stock.**	• Check out your classroom: How big is it? What shape? • Note the locations of windows, doors, smartboards/whiteboards, cabinets, and electrical outlets. • What kind of seating and furniture is already in your classroom? • What materials are available that could be repurposed/recycled or thrown out?
STEP 2 **Consider the three key design elements.**	• Naturalness: How will you bring nature into the space? • Individualization: How will you tailor the space to meet the needs of your students? • Stimulation: How will you strike a balance between *too much* and *not enough*?
STEP 3 **Set goals.**	• What is your primary goal for your classroom environment? (Create a strong sense of community? Foster student independence? Ensure accessibility?) • What is your secondary goal?

Goals for my space!

Your answers to these questions will help you clarify your vision. In a few pages, you'll have the opportunity to apply your answers when you sketch a classroom layout that aligns with your goals and supports your students' needs.

CHARACTERISTICS OF EFFECTIVE, FUNCTIONAL LEARNING SPACES

Two classrooms can look quite different from one another and yet meet the needs of the students and teachers who work there. Although classroom layout and design choices may differ, most functional learning spaces share the following common characteristics:

✳ **Flexible** Furniture and seating arrangements can be easily moved to accommodate different activities.

✳ **Accessible** Students of all abilities can independently navigate the space and reach needed materials.

✳ **Equitable** All students have equal access to class materials and resources, and seating arrangements de-emphasize student social status while providing opportunities for peer interaction (Wilkins et al., 2023).

✳ **Comfortable** Students (and visitors) feel welcome. The room isn't too bright or dim, loud or quiet, or hot or cool, and learners have access to tools (such as noise-canceling headphones) that they can use to moderate sensory input.

✳ **Engaging** Interesting décor inspires curiosity but doesn't overwhelm the senses.

✳ **Practical** The space supports both the teacher and learners in accomplishing their shared goals. You may see content anchor charts, reminders of class routines and norms, and community-building displays highlighting student interests and achievements, as well as designated areas for collaboration and solo work.

Eddie Vitcavage uses his Focus Wall as a reference point for students. They can easily see the big ideas, key skills, and vocabulary they're working on in each subject area.

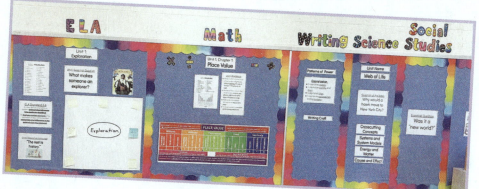

 Which of these characteristics currently apply to your classroom? Which need work? Brainstorm one or two things you can do to make your space more effective.

CREATE A STUDENT-FRIENDLY SPACE

These ideas weave in the six characteristics of effective classroom spaces you just read about.

Self-Serve Center

Stock an easily accessible space with materials students need and encourage them to help themselves. Tim Wheeler's self-serve center includes:

⭐ **Community crayons, pens, pencils, and erasers** "If somebody loses their blue crayon, this is where they can borrow one," Tim says. "Toward the end of the year, I add eraser tops because we start having lots of pencils with no erasers."

⭐ **Bandages** Instead of managing every minor request for a bandage, Tim allows students to help themselves.*

⭐ **Various kinds of writing paper** Students can choose which type of paper they prefer for open-ended writing assignments, including paper with a space for both drawing and writing and notebook-style paper. ("The paper students choose tells me something about them and their needs," Tim says.)

⭐ **Graphic organizers** Students can choose the one that suits their needs.

⭐ **Self-paced assignments** Students who finish assigned work early can choose from a variety of activities, including educational puzzles and a self-paced playwriting course. (Students working on that course also have access to Tim's puppets to rehearse, revise, and perform their writing!)

*Yes, students may occasionally take more than they need. Setting clear expectations for material use—and reminding students of their responsibility as members of the class community—helps mitigate overuse.

Sharpened pencils in one cup; dull pencils in the other (Sharpening pencils is a class job.)

Community crayons, pens, pencils, and erasers

Various kinds of writing paper and graphic organizers

Bandages and first aid kit

"My self-serve center multiplies me because it enables me to help more kids."

—TIM WHEELER, third-grade teacher

Calm Corner

Set up at least one cozy space where students can decompress as needed. Consider adding some comfy seating, soft pillows or stuffed animals, tactile sensory items (like stress balls or fidget toys), quiet activities (like coloring pages and crayons), and a poster outlining stress reduction activities (like deep breathing). If possible, include tools students can use to control and manage sensory input, such as noise-reducing headphones and an eye mask.

"This year, I'm going to have two calm corners, so if students get into a conflict, both will have access to resources in a different space."

—EDDIE VITCAVAGE, fifth-grade teacher

Sherri Amos sets up a supportive spot for her fourth graders to cool down. It includes a comfy seat, a fish tank, a sand timer, and posters with reminders and tips about cooling down.

Student Showcase

Designate a spot of honor for student creations, including artwork, stories, and inventions. Encourage students to bring in photos, objects, and certificates that celebrate their out-of-school activities as well. Of course, you can also feature outstanding student assignments.

Some simple display ideas: Staple a few clear plastic sheet protectors to a bulletin board so you can quickly swap out pictures, writing, and drawings. Put up a "clothesline" and use clothespins or binder clips to hang student work.

Rotate displays regularly, making sure every student is represented and celebrated equally throughout the year.

Katie Kim highlights two parts of her fifth graders' reports using a traditional display overlaid with banners of covers attached with paper clips to clotheslines.

Katie staples clear plastic sheet protectors to a bulletin board to easily swap out pictures, writing, and drawings.

CLASSROOM LAYOUTS: PROS & CONS

Three sketches from Eddie Vitcavage, BreAnn Fennell, and Valente' Gibson capture different layouts.

Desks/Tables in Rows

The classic classroom layout:

- **Great for** Lectures, independent work, and teacher-centered instruction
- **Not good for** Collaborative work and peer communication. Can make group activities and discussion challenging.

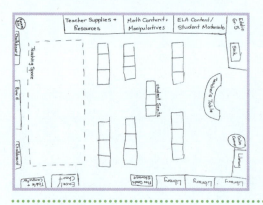

Pair or Group Seating

Desk (or tables) arranged in small groups of 2, 3, or 4:

- **Great for** Collaborative work and peer discussion. Supports shared learning and encourages teamwork.
- **Not good for** Independent work, test-taking

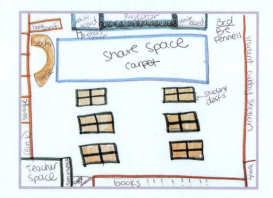

U- or V-shape

Seating arranged around an open area:

- **Great for** Demonstrations, class discussions, and interactive lessons
- **Not good for** Large classes, independent work

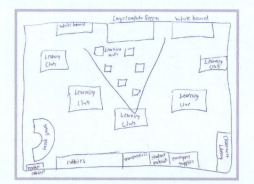

Watch this!

Michele Ogden shows how she's designed seating for various purposes, such as small-group work.

PRACTICAL DÉCOR

Your classroom doesn't have to be picture-perfect. Function is more important than aesthetics! Simple, sensory-friendly decor helps students of all abilities thrive. Use these tips, initially developed to help teachers meet the needs of students with autism spectrum disorder, to create a neurodiverse-friendly environment:

"You are going to spend a lot of time in your classroom, so make it feel like a second home."
—HANNAH KITTLE, fifth-grade teacher

- ✯ **Use the front wall to display daily materials,** such as a calendar, schedule, or a word wall.

- ✯ **Align wall displays with the current topic,** so that if students' attention wanders, they've got visual anchors with relevant information around them.

- ✯ **Use book covers to highlight learning.** Take books that feature topics students are reading about or favorite read-alouds and stand them on shelves, a windowsill, or any ledge in the room.

- ✯ **Minimize excessive sensory input.** Use shades and carpet to minimize glare from classroom windows; turn off overhead fluorescent lights and opt for less intense and less direct lighting as needed (Martin & Wilkins, 2021).

Hannah's "flags of the world" string banners welcome her multilingual students into the room, but are placed high overhead. What students see at eye-level during instruction are simply decorated walls (with spaces in the back reserved for their work). Shades prevent glare from the sun, while allowing in natural light.

Connect & Reflect

Use the space below to sketch out a classroom design.*

DOWNLOAD HERE!

 PUT IT ALL TOGETHER!

In addition to existing equipment/furniture that cannot be moved, be sure to include:

☐ Student seating

☐ Community gathering area

☐ Student self-serve center

☐ Book nook or library

☐ Shelves/areas for other materials students need to access

☐ Calm corner

☐ Teacher space

☐ Storage

☐ Space for a Student Showcase

*Prefer to use technology? Search online for "seating chart maker."

OUTFITTING WITHOUT OVERSPENDING

Don't break the bank to outfit your classroom! While it's true that many teachers use personal funds to enhance their classrooms (sometimes up to $1,000!), you don't have to tap your bank account to create an engaging learning environment. Try these ideas instead:

✳ **Share and swap with other educators.** Share your needs and wants with your colleagues. Much of what you need may already be in the building. "I didn't have fraction manipulatives in my classroom, but down the hall, another teacher had two sets," says Eddie Vitcavage, fifth-grade teacher.

✳ **Use free resources.** Check online marketplaces and local Buy Nothing groups. You can also request donations of needed supplies, such as gently used lamps, rugs, and storage bins. And don't forget free online tools that can help you create bulletin-board décor, posters, and learning materials.

✳ **Recycle.** Get creative! What can you reuse or repurpose? Clean food containers (think cans and plastic jars) can be used to store markers or paint brushes; old pillowcases can be turned into back-of-chair covers that include pockets for extra storage.

✳ **Apply for grants.** Some school PTAs and community organizations offer grants to teachers. Ask your colleagues to fill you in on available opportunities.

Did you know...?
The IRS allows educators to deduct up to $300 if they spend personal funds on classroom items like books, supplies, and equipment. Save your receipts—and always check with a tax professional before claiming deductions (IRS, 2024).

THINK What's your first stop for free or cheap classroom furniture and décor? Which of these options will you explore?

Check Out This Book!

The Commonsense Guide to Your Classroom Library

Want expert advice on setting up a classroom library you and your students will use and love? Book-access advocates Donalyn Miller and Colby Sharp show you how to acquire no-cost and low-cost books that work best for your students, as well as how to organize and maintain your collection, create check-out routines, and more.

REARRANGE AS NEEDED!

Just as you may need to redo your routines in response to new situations, you may need to rearrange (or redecorate) your space to better fit the needs of your class. Consider rearranging if you can answer "yes" to any of these questions:

QUESTION	YES	NO
Are you tired of your current setup? Simple changes can re-energize a space—and its occupants!	☐	☐
Have your students' interests changed? Students grow a lot during a school year. Switch out student-centric décor to reflect their evolving interests.	☐	☐
Are any of your students struggling to navigate the space? Enlist your students to help you figure out how to make your room more accessible.	☐	☐
Have you noticed a lot of wasted time? Poor design and difficult-to-reach supplies may be part of the problem.	☐	☐
Are your students frequently overwhelmed or frustrated? Simplifying your classroom may help.	☐	☐

"I adjust my space almost every day, such as by moving a student who's having trouble staying focused to a different seat. My latest adjustment? Moving headphones in the listening center from a bucket to a shoe organizer to prevent the cords from tangling—a big time-saver!"

—MORGAN MERCADO, third-grade teacher

Consider adding "re-evaluate classroom layout" reminders to your calendar. End-of-quarter and holiday breaks are good times to review and rearrange, if needed.

TIME & SPACE SEND-OFF

Whew...more tips and tools for keeping your classroom running smoothly!

Big Ideas to Keep in Mind

⭐ You can handle a LOT, but you can't do it all. Create a calendar that includes time for daily responsibilities and important things that are outside of instructional time, like staff meetings, personal matters, and family events!

⭐ To keep your workload manageable, set boundaries, delegate tasks, and collaborate with colleagues and families to help you find time-saving solutions.

⭐ Build breaks (and fun!) into class time to prime students' brains and support their well-being—and yours! (Build in your own breaks, too!)

⭐ Design the "best" classroom layout for this year's students—and that means it will evolve over time and likely won't be perfect at first.

⭐ Ask yourself how students are using the space at different times, and if they all have equitable access to tools and materials. Be ready to make adjustments.

⭐ Your classroom is a reflection of you and your students, so personalize the space to create a welcoming environment for everyone—students, families, and you!

Eddie Vitcavage shares this bit of wisdom with new teachers: "Your classroom will be radically different from all other classrooms because you don't have the same students or same resources as any other class. Do what works for you and your students."

THERE IS A PLACE FOR EVERYONE IN OUR CLASSROOM

Here, we make space to spark learning, new ideas, and friendships.

Here's a quote you can display to prompt discussion with students about their classroom community.

PART 3

RELATIONSHIPS

NURTURING CONNECTIONS & BUILDING CONFIDENCE

When he was teaching fifth grade, Valente' Gibson often ate lunch with his students. "I'd intentionally sit with or near the students who were not interested in school, just to get to know them," Valente' says.

"After I'd spend a few weeks getting to know the student, I'd call the parent and say something like, 'I really enjoy getting to know little Johnny. One thing I really love is that he...' and then there'd

Kindergarten teacher Tiffany Young-Norris connects with a student at her cheerleading event.

be a shift in the parent as they realized I've been intentionally trying to get to know their child."

Third-grade teacher Michele Ogden and her co-workers use a spreadsheet to facilitate the same kind of special staff-student relationship. "The spreadsheet helps me remember each of my students' likes, dislikes, and interests," says Michele. "If I'm not connecting with a student, despite my efforts, I'll ask a colleague who shares some similar interests to spend time with that student. We strive to ensure that every student in our school has at least one adult that they feel comfortable with."

Building relationships with students, staff, and families is foundational to every teacher's success—you'll find it's an investment in the well-being of each student, and in the entire classroom community.

LET'S BEGIN

Teachers who care about their students—beyond their grades—and who encourage and support their students typically have fewer disciplinary problems in their classroom, and the students often do better academically (Hawkins et al., 2001; Li & Julian, 2012).

Why? When teachers think about what's developmentally appropriate for kids and apply it to their instruction, kids learn better. This includes thinking about their:

* Ages
* Social and emotional needs
* Skills
* Attention spans
* Motivations

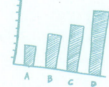

It may seem impossible to develop that kind of relationship with each child in your classroom. There's only one of you, many of them, and a long list of academic content you're expected to cover. But you don't have to do it alone—and a little effort goes a long way. The following sections share quick tips with big payoffs.

In this section, you'll learn:

☆ How to forge strong relationships with each of your students

☆ Effective strategies to communicate with families

☆ Why relationships are critical to student success

☆ How to collaborate with colleagues

☆ How to boost student confidence and competence

☆ Techniques to bolster your confidence

Your name	What do you like to do for fun?	What is challenging for you?	What would you like to learn about this year in school?	What types of books do you like reading?	What's your favorite food?	TEACHER PAIRING
Alex	Read	Math	Science	Chapter books	Pasta	
Sofia	Play soccer	Cursive	Fractions	Minecraft	Pizza/ramen	Ms. Yon
Marcos	Ride bikes	Something I've never done	Everything	Magic Treehouse	Sushi	Mrs. Reyes
Justin	Watch my favorite sports team	Chinese	Multiplication	What in the Now	Ramen	Mrs. McManus
Ana Lucia	Annoy my brothers	Making friends	Algebra	Manga	Chicken nuggets and fries	Mrs. Reyes
Christian	Go for a walk	Arm wrestling	Division	Big Nate	Dumplings	Mr. Arts
Michael	Make a fort with my sister	Division	Math	One Piece	Burgers	Mrs. McManus
Yasmin	Video games	Word problems	Music	Funny books	Bameya	Ms. Yon
						Mr. Thomas

Using results from a student-interest survey helps Michele Ogden and her team match individual students with staff members who get to know them throughout the year—a strong social-emotional safety net!

CONNECTIONS

CONNECTIONS 101

School connectedness—the degree to which students and their families feel positively connected to school—not only affects student learning, it also affects their health and well-being. Over the course of the year, you'll have a huge impact on how students (and their families) feel about school and learning. As you consider strategies for building developmental relationships on the following pages, what follows are some questions to keep in mind:

Will what I do support students'

* **Emotional connection?** Strong relationships are built on care, trust, and emotional support.
* **Progressive growth?** Together, teachers and students tackle increasingly more difficult tasks, with the teacher providing support and encouragement.
* **Shifting independence?** Over time, students will handle more and more tasks independently (Li & Julian, 2012).

Did you know...?
Students who feel connected to school are more likely to make healthy choices—and avoid risky behaviors, like substance use and violence (CDC, 2022).

"Kids are more apt to listen to people who care about them."

—BREANN FENNELL, third-grade teacher

FORGING STRONG RELATIONSHIPS WITH STUDENTS

Here are five research-backed principles to apply as you forge strong relationships with your students:

1 Express care.

Be dependable, listen, demonstrate belief in your students' skills and potential, be warm, and encourage learners.

2 Encourage growth.

Let students know you expect their best, and push them to stretch beyond their current capability. Hold them accountable for their actions and help them learn from their mistakes.

3 Provide support.

Establish and enforce boundaries and limits, build students' confidence and competence, advocate for them as needed, and help them navigate challenges.

4 Share power.

Treat learners with respect, involve them in classroom decisions and goal setting, and give students opportunities to lead.

5 Expand possibilities.

Expose students to new ideas, experiences, and people. Connect them with others who can help them grow.

Did you know...? Teacher caring and support are associated with improved student engagement in math and reading (Kearney et al., 2014).

Remember what I said about personalized morning greetings (page 16)? Routines and norms can be superpower management tools that show you value students, while providing them with safety and structure throughout the day. (See Part 1 for more ideas.)

Have you organized a self-serve center (page 68) or made materials more accessible for kids in other ways? The way you use space and effectively use your time can provide kids with the support they need to feel comfortable and self-reliant in your room. (See Part 2 for more ideas.)

HOW TO SAY IT

Words can inspire and build connections—or silence and distance students. Choose your words wisely and apologize and reframe them if you've said something you regret. (See Repairing Relationships, page 97.) Students respect your effort and intention when they know their well-being is your highest priority. Consider these common examples on the next page for starters.

As you select your words, consider how you can invite students to respond in a comfortable way. Keep in mind that some children are chatty, but some hesitate to speak up in groups. And some prefer to connect nonverbally. Be sure you use multiple modes of communication, including writing or drawing, digital surveys, and even private conversations—and give students lots of options to connect with you.

"My students love hearing their home language, Spanish. When we play translation games, they flip the game on me and try to give me the most complex English sentences they can think of to test my Spanish skills—a win-win for everyone learning both languages!"

—**BRIDGET JORDAN,** ESOL teacher

Bridget Jordan finds clever ways to connect with students throughout the day, including their favorite quiet signal, "llama lockdown," shown here. Students know all things Peru are Bridget's passion! Another attention signal, "Freeze like a *paleta* [popsicle]!", has become a class joke as students try to catch each other "unfrozen."

Check Out This Book!

The Words That Shape Us

A former teacher and SEL consultant shares classroom-tested strategies and brain-changing language you can use to transform how students think, feel, and achieve within their classroom community and beyond.

HOW TO SAY IT

CHALLENGE	WISE WORDS IN RESPONSE
Students aren't making friends easily.	What do you think makes you a good friend? I'll share first....
Students don't listen and/or respond to one another's ideas in a discussion.	To keep our brains learning and coming up with new ideas, let's respond to each other with one of these sentence starters: *I liked what you said about _____ because _____.* *I agree/disagree about _____ because _____.* *When you said _____, I wondered _____.* *Could you explain what you meant by _____?*
A student seems reluctant to try a new activity/assignment.	Why is this challenging for you?
Students are anxious about trying new things and are failing or are embarrassed by mistakes.	Mistakes help us learn; thank you for that opportunity. **TIP:** Social-emotional learning coach and teacher educator Lily Scott recommends making this a class motto: "We make brilliant mistakes" (Scott, 2025).
A student makes an off-topic comment that could derail a lesson or discussion.	I would love to talk to you about this later. Can you remind me when we're heading out to recess?

"When I started teaching, I thought, 'We have to get this work done' and shut down personal conversations with students. Now, I know that those conversations can help me make connections—and I make time for them."

—MICHELE OGDEN, third-grade teacher

Connect & Reflect

Use this rating scale to identify your strengths in communicating with students and making opportunities to connect with them more deeply. For each statement, choose the answer that best reflects your current practice.

DOWNLOAD HERE!

 BOOST YOUR CONNECTION SKILLS

CONNECTION TARGETS	NOT YET	SOMETIMES	OFTEN
I set high expectations for my students and encourage them to meet them.	☐	☐	☐
I take my students' personalities and interests into account when planning lessons.	☐	☐	☐
I learn about my students' favorite pastimes and hobbies and share info about my interests and hobbies.	☐	☐	☐
I can handle a bit of opposition from students and use it as a learning moment.	☐	☐	☐
I'm comfortable admitting mistakes to my students when appropriate.	☐	☐	☐
I make time to talk about topics that are important to my students.	☐	☐	☐
I help students organize their work and catch up if they've been absent or need extra support.	☐	☐	☐
I take a personal interest in my students' lives beyond academics.	☐	☐	☐

☐ **Now,** take a moment to reflect first on your strengths: What are you doing "often" that works well? How does it help set the tone for healthy relationships?

☐ **Next,** review your areas for progress. Look for the statements where you checked "sometimes." Are there any opportunities to make a relationship-building action more regular or frequent? For instance, if you're sometimes comfortable admitting mistakes to students, you might set a goal of letting students hear you talk through a mistake at least once a week —and celebrate the learning when you do.

☐ **Finally,** look for the statements where you checked "not yet." Pick just one to start working on, and set small, achievable goals to improve. For example, if you're not yet making time to talk about topics important to your students, try setting aside a few minutes each day to ask open-ended questions or discuss their interests.

> This process will help you build on your strengths while working steadily on areas that need improvement, one step at a time.

BEFORE SCHOOL BEGINS

Send a welcome note to students and families. Introduce yourself, let your students know how excited you are to meet them, and share some basic information about what to expect on the first day.

First-grade teacher Kevin Frederick sends a letter to families to introduce himself, along with a survey they can complete to help him learn more about his students.

At Open House, Tiffany Young-Norris gives each student an "Invite Mrs. Norris" request form and tells them "I really like to see what my students are doing outside of school, so you can invite me to any event of your choosing." To date, she's attended ballet recitals, soccer games, family reunions, and birthday parties—all of which help her connect with students' extended families and communities.

Tiffany Young-Norris attends a student's birthday party.

Her invitation sets some helpful parameters for families, including asking her to attend an event at least a month in advance.

FIRST WEEKS OF SCHOOL

Establish connections with fun getting-to-know-you activities:

Name Stories

Sharing name stories is a powerful way to build relationships, while practicing classroom norms and learning more about one another's cultures. Valente' Gibson, an afterschool coordinator who previously taught fifth grade, reads a book to his class to start the conversation.

After reading, Valente' asks his students: "Is it fair for people to mispronounce names or give you a nickname because they don't want to say your name?" This leads to a discussion about their own names: *Do you like your name? Do you know where it came from?*

Next, the class brainstorms questions they can ask to discover their name stories. (*Who named me? How did I get my name?*) Students then interview family members and share their stories with the class a few days later.

"One year, we made a class book with our name stories," Valente' says. "We also invited families to share their name stories at an Open House night."

***Alma and How She Got Her Name,* by Juana Martinez-Neal** Alma Sofia Esperanza José Pura Candela wonders why her name is so long, until she hears her father's explanation: each name honors an ancestor with a unique story. As she listens, she discovers the power of a name and dreams of adding to its meaning.

***The Name Jar,* by Yangsook Choi** It's Unhei's first day of school, and no one can pronounce her name. She decides to pick an American name from a jar—but none of them feel right. With help from a friend, Unhei learns to embrace her Korean name.

***Your Name Is a Song,* by Jamilah Thompkins-Bigelow** After hearing her name mispronounced by her teachers and peers, a young girl's mother shows her the lyricism of different cultural names. With a new appreciation for her name, she feels ready to return to school and share what she's learned.

***Hey L'il D!: It's All in the Name,* by Heather Goodyear & Bob Lanier** L'il D and his friends offer to help the new kid, Gan, find a nickname that fits. This story explores the many ways nicknames shape identity— for better or worse— and the power in embracing who you are.

All About Me

Kindergarten teacher Tiffany Young-Norris uses a tactile show-and-tell-style activity to learn more about her students. First, she creates what she calls an "All About Me" bag: a brown paper lunch bag stuffed with a few representative objects.

"Last year, mine had a pink headband with a crayon on it because my favorite color is pink and I like to dress up; a tiny cow logo from my favorite fast-food restaurant; a picture of my previous class because I love my students; and a picture of my dog," she says. She shares her bag and stories with students during Circle Time, and then gives each child a bag (with instructions stapled to the front) to fill at home. Students take turns sharing their "All About Me" bags with the class over the next few days.

Sharing items from their "All About Me" bags invites Tiffany Young-Norris's kindergartners to delight in learning about their teacher and one another.

FOUR THINGS ABOUT ME

Put the spotlight on yourself and let your students use their sleuthing skills to establish connections. Third-grade teacher BreAnn Fennell challenges students to guess four facts about her, based on context clues.

"Sometimes they'll say, 'I bet you really like to read' because I have so many books in my classroom, or 'she probably loves owls' because I have some owl decorations displayed," BreAnn says. "And sometimes they'll guess my favorite color is whatever color shirt I'm wearing."

This activity doesn't simply give BreAnn an opportunity to introduce herself to her students, it also underscores the importance of conversation to identify and check assumptions.

THROUGHOUT THE YEAR

Create regular times for sharing and conversation.

Good News Monday

First-grade teacher Kevin Frederick helps kids ease back into classroom routines with Good News Monday. "In our sharing circle on Monday, they get to share something they did over the weekend, something they're really excited about, or something good that happened at home or school," Kevin says. Those glimpses of students' outside-of-school lives help Kevin and his class connect.

Class Time = Family Time

Former teacher Valente' Gibson called his class's morning gathering "Family Time" and encouraged students to share and discuss topics of interest during that time. (He always came prepared in case students didn't introduce a subject. A favorite discussion prompt: *What's your favorite song?*)

Valente' Gibson's fifth graders gather on the rug to discuss their understandings about an article they've selected during Family Time.

After reading his first piece of the year, a student author signs the Author Chair (an old chair BreAnn Fennell has painted with chalkboard paint).

Author Chair

Early in the school year, BreAnn Fennell introduces a special seat of honor that gives its occupant the opportunity to share their writing uninterrupted. During the first week of school, students take turns sharing their "About Me" stories (and practicing good listening skills). Students sign the chair after reading their work, and the Author Chair becomes a beloved part of the class culture.

PARTNERING WITH FAMILIES

Be Positive

Your first interaction with a student's family should never be negative. Get off to a great start by proactively reaching out to families to tell them what you enjoy about working with their child. When you provide specific details, you assure families that you will take the time to notice their child carefully—and will be able to back up future observations with facts: *Tristan's really been kind to others in our class. He noticed a classmate was really sad about losing her dog and offered to talk with her at lunch since he'd lost a pet, too.*

Positive communications like this reassure parents that you see the good in their child—and set the stage for ongoing communication and cooperation.

Set Boundaries

Your students' caregivers need to know how to reach you, but you can (and should!) establish boundaries to determine:

⭐ **When will you be available?** Decide when you're available for family communications and share that schedule. You're not required to respond to emails on weekends or after school hours, unless you choose to.

⭐ **How can caregivers reach you?** Let families know the best way to contact you. (By email? Text? Phone? App?) Offer alternative ways to stay in touch if needed.

⭐ **What can families expect from you?** Clarify how quickly you'll respond. Set a reasonable time frame (e.g., within 24–48 hours) and let families know what steps to take if they don't hear back within that window.

SPOTLIGHT ON FAMILY CONNECTIONS

"Lead with empathy and assume positive intentions from everybody."

—KEVIN FREDERICK,
first-grade teacher

Check Out This Book!

Everyone Wins! The Evidence for Family-School Partnerships and Implications for Practice

Engaging families not only improves student achievement, but also strengthens families, boosts teacher effectiveness, and builds community. This guide shows educators how to design and implement research-based family-engagement programs with confidence.

"Sometimes I'd be at a local cafe, and sometimes a fast-food place. And I'd usually have on jeans or some chill clothes, so they'd see me in a different light. Some families see teachers as authority figures, but outside of school, we're on the same level."

—VALENTE' GIBSON,
afterschool coordinator

Get Creative

Phone calls, emails, and text messages are the mainstays of teacher-parent communication these days but remember, not all families have the same availability or access. It's important to meet families where they are. Creative efforts to connect can strengthen trust and increase engagement. Here are some ideas:

✳ **Work in the community.** Valente' Gibson made it a point to grade papers (or work on lesson plans) at a local business one Saturday morning each month—and told families they were welcome to stop in and say hi.

✳ **Send photo-heavy newsletters.** Parents love to see what their child is doing at school. Photos of kids working together and having fun can ease family anxiety and spark parent-child conversations.

✳ **Include tips to encourage conversation.** Incorporating conversation prompts into social media posts and newsletters helps parents talk to their kids about what they're learning at school (Mapp et al., 2022).

✳ **Record and share short videos.** Some caregivers can't get to school. Share video tours and special moments.

Did you know…?
Teacher-family communication can increase student engagement. One study found that regular phone calls home increased homework completion and class participation (Kraft & Dougherty, 2012).

BEST PRACTICES FOR FAMILY COMMUNICATION

DO	DON'T
Use clear, simple language.	Use educational jargon.
Account for home languages: Involve a translator or use digital translation tools to communicate with families.	Use English-only communications or ask students to serve as translators.
Address communications to "families" or "caregivers."	Use "parents" or "mom and dad" in your initial family communication. Some children live with grandparents or guardians; some have two moms or no mom.
Express your belief that the student will have a successful year.	Expect that students or families who've had negative school experiences in the past will have a bad year.
Highlight student strengths.	Let other teachers' comments or past reports color your perception of a child or family.
Clearly communicate your role and desire to partner with the family.	Approach communication as a one-way street where you're the expert.
Tell families what they can do to help students succeed in school.	Assume that families understand the importance of regular school attendance.
Share academic details and behavioral observations with families regularly.	Only contact families when there are problems or concerns.
Invite families into your classroom, and find alternative ways to involve caregivers whose work schedules or transportation options may not allow them to participate during school hours.	Believe that families who don't attend school events are uninterested in their child's education.
Ask how you can help them meet their goals for their child.	Assume you are meeting families' educational expectations.

Did you know...?
Research shows that the trust and connections between schools, students, families, and communities have 3–5 times more impact on math and reading achievement than funding alone (Salloum et al., 2018).

Connect & Reflect

Using a script can make family phone calls easier—and more productive. Here's a template you can use or adapt.

DOWNLOAD HERE!

 ## POSITIVE PHONE-CALL SCRIPT

TOPIC	NOTES
1 Introduce yourself. EXAMPLE: *Hi, Mrs. Lopez. I'm Miss Smith and I'm Sofia's teacher this year. I'm calling to introduce myself.*	
2 Welcome the family as part of your class. EXAMPLE: *I'm so happy to have Sofia in my class this year, and I look forward to meeting and learning more about you and the rest of your family.*	
3 Express the importance of partnership. EXAMPLE: *I believe that working together is the best way to help Sofia thrive.*	
4 Conversation starter: Share a positive story or observation to learn something new. EXAMPLE: *I love Sofia's curiosity—she asks such great questions in class! What kinds of things does she like to explore at home?*	
5 Establish the best times and methods of communication. EXAMPLE: *I know you're a busy person. What's the best way for me to connect with you this year? Do you prefer emails, phone calls, or texts?*	
6 Thank you and closing EXAMPLE: *It's been a pleasure getting to know you. Do you have any questions for me? How can I support you?*	

BUILD YOUR PROFESSIONAL NETWORK

You may be assigned a teacher mentor. Or mentorships at your school may be more informal. Whether you have access to a formal mentorship or not, you can benefit tremendously from the support and wisdom of experienced educators.
You can find it in two places:

① In your school

Solid relationships with the teachers and paraprofessionals you work with every day will serve you well. These are the people who understand the school culture, know your students, and can pitch in when you need help. In-house mentors can often provide specific advice because they know you and the environment you're working in.

Here's how to connect:

⭐ Participate in school events and activities, including social gatherings, non-mandatory meetings, and student extracurriculars.

⭐ Extend an invitation. Ask a colleague if they'd like to have lunch with you or grab coffee during a shared break.

⭐ Set a regular check-in time with a mentor or grade-level colleague. You can use it to plan, grade, or ask advice on handling academic or behavior challenges.

"I wouldn't have survived my first couple of years teaching without my mentors. Surround yourself with them and other people that you trust."
—**KEVIN FREDERICK,** first-grade teacher

During orientation, staff members at BreAnn Fennell's school each decorated a trucker hat with patches to match their personality. Here, she poses with her student teacher, Kelsey Kinsley. She says, "It was exciting to see what everyone picked, and we enjoyed talking and bonding as we ironed on our creations."

❷ Externally

Connecting with educators outside of your school or district will help you expand your professional network and give you access to fresh perspectives, innovative teaching strategies, and diverse resources. Here's how to connect:

✳ **Join online teacher communities.** Use platforms such as LinkedIn, blogs, and social media forums to connect (and share ideas with) educators worldwide.

✳ **Attend conferences and educational workshops.** Search "teacher conferences near me" (or wherever you'd like to go) to uncover a variety of options. Your state Department of Public Instruction and professional organizations likely offer in-person and online events as well, providing ample opportunities to meet fellow educators.

Ideally, you'll develop strong connections both within your school and with the broader educational community.

Scholastic's Innovation Lab offers an opportunity to collaborate with students, teachers, and administrators to co-design education solutions. Participants will help shape new products and programs throughout the development process—from the initial discovery phase to testing and workshopping—and will expand their network.

SUPPORT STAFF, SPECIALISTS, AND ADMIN

Building good relationships with your principal, custodians, school nurse, learning specialists, and other staff members can make your job easier and more enjoyable. Each of these individuals also contributes to the success of your students, so be sure to say "hi" and "thank you" when appropriate. Greet them by name, show interest in their lives, and learn how you can help them succeed at work.

Simple measures, like placing your trash can in the designated spot at the end of the day and proactively sharing academic info with math interventionists, enable your colleagues to do their jobs more effectively—which ultimately benefits you and your students as well.

"Teaching can be isolating if you close your door and try to do everything yourself."

—HANNAH KITTLE, fifth-grade teacher

SIX FRIENDS EVERY TEACHER NEEDS

1 Veteran sage

A teacher who's been on the job for a while and has seen teaching trends come and go. Flustered by nothing, the "veteran sage" offers perspective and insider tips to help you navigate school culture.

2 Fellow newbie

It helps to know you're not the only one struggling! Sharing experiences with another new teacher can help you navigate the ups and downs of a career non-teachers may not understand.

3 180° partner

Someone who's radically different from you, perhaps in terms of background, subject, or teaching philosophy. You'll learn a lot by interacting with someone who approaches teaching through another lens (Hubbard, 2023).

4 360° partner

A teacher who's very similar to you in terms of background and interests. Your shared experiences will help you connect (Hubbard, 2023).

5 Tech enthusiast

They love trying out the latest ed tech and have recommendations for what works (and what doesn't) in the classroom. This is the person you go to when you can't figure out a tech tool or are looking for a way to streamline your tasks.

6 Got-your-back buddy

A compassionate, caring educator who won't judge you and will listen when you need to vent. Because sometimes, you need a hug and reassurance to make it through the afternoon!

Keke Powell draws on the expertise of veteran colleagues like Ms. Miller to plan units. Their collaboration increases the quality of their lessons and the number of resources and ideas to draw on—plus, it can be fun to work together!

FOUR PEOPLE TO AVOID

1 Gabby gossip

You don't need to know the details of anyone's personal life. And remember: A colleague who's spilling the tea about a co-worker is unlikely to keep your secrets, so be careful what you share!

2 Constant complainer

Focusing on the negatives can suck all your time and energy. Politely excuse yourself from conversations that dwell on complaints without offering solutions; spend more time with the problem-solvers than with those who endlessly point out problems.

3 Apathetic one

Don't let an educator who gave up long ago dampen your desire to make a difference. You may hear cynicism about new initiatives—after all, experienced teachers have seen a lot of educational trends come and go—but stay grounded. When others say, "What's the point?," remind yourself that small efforts can have a big impact.

4 Micromanager

There's more than one right way to do just about everything. When a micromanaging colleague offers unsolicited advice, you don't have to follow it. A polite but firm response could be, "Thanks for the suggestion, but I've got a plan that works for me." Things are a bit trickier if the micromanager is your mentor or boss. Try saying, "I appreciate your guidance, and I'd love to talk through how I can incorporate your feedback while still making it my own."

"At first, it's hard to tell which colleagues will help you and those who may not share your commitment to students and to improving your practice. At a new school, I find it's best to express your concerns, struggles, and feelings to either your department chair, head teacher, or mentor. With time, you will know who you can trust and who you cannot."

—MILAGROS SANCHEZ-COHEN, kindergarten teacher

Connect & Reflect

Here's a quick exercise to target the support
you need most right now.

DOWNLOAD HERE!

 ## STRENGTHENING PROFESSIONAL RELATIONSHIPS

REFLECT: What type of professional support do I most need right now?

- ☐ Strategies to engage students
- ☐ Constructive feedback from peers or mentors
- ☐ A listening ear to provide emotional support
- ☐ Other:

- ☐ Ideas for adapting lessons to meet diverse learning needs
- ☐ Help identifying and addressing learning or behavioral challenges for one or more students

_____

_____

BRAINSTORM: How can I get it? Where could I find it?

- ☐ Observe a colleague's class
- ☐ Schedule regular check-ins with a mentor
- ☐ Attend a conference or professional learning workshop
- ☐ Other:

- ☐ Join a teacher support group
- ☐ Engage in an online teacher community
- ☐ Invite another teacher to lunch/coffee
- ☐ Request feedback from your principal

_____

_____

GET SPECIFIC: What exactly will you do to address your challenge?
Who will you reach out to?

EXAMPLE: I will attend the Future of EdTech & Learning Conference to get ideas for interactive review games; I will ask Mr. Jamerson if I can observe his class to watch how he manages the rest of the class when meeting with small groups.

I will _____ to _____

_____

_____

SCHEDULE IT: Put it on your calendar!

CONNECTING WITH HARD-TO-REACH HUMANS

As a teacher, you regularly interact with humans of various ages, backgrounds, and abilities. Some you'll connect with easily. With others, you'll find that your usual approaches don't work. Don't give up. Often, those who are hardest to reach are those who most need connection.

Try a Different Approach, One-on-One

Adjust the timing, content, and delivery of your communications. For example, if a student shuts down and turns away every time you attempt a conversation, try sitting together in silence. Or do something together—draw a picture, toss a ball. Persist as needed.

Discuss or Role-Play to Build Social Skills

Helping students understand social norms and make good decisions in challenging situations develops their social and emotional awareness. This may be especially helpful for harder-to-reach kids who can work through social scenarios without being the focus of attention.

Build time into whole-class meetings for students to talk out or role-play challenging situations (e.g., when students won't sit with the new kid at lunch, when someone borrows a favorite pencil and breaks it, or when friends disagree about rules in a recess game). You may want to start this work frequently, as students are learning norms and routines (see Part 1), and then transition to a weekly or twice-weekly basis, as students begin to demonstrate appropriate behaviors and make healthy, considerate decisions.

"If you are having disciplinary problems with a student, commit to talking to that kid for five minutes, one-on-one, five days in a row—about anything other than school."

—TIM WHEELER, third-grade teacher

How to Say Sorry
Dominique and Amanda got into an argument at school. Amanda said she didn't like Dominique's favorite band. Later, both of them realized that their argument was silly. Still, each friend thought the other should be the first to apologize.

Talk/Write About
- Have you ever had an argument with a friend and realized that it really wasn't worth fighting over? How did you resolve your conflict?

Not Making the Grade
Luis and his best friend, Sean, are doing a history project. Luis does more work than Sean. He complains

Late Report
Andrew has a book report due tomorrow. His teacher assigned it last week. But he does not begin reading his book until the night before it's due. He knows he won't have time to finish the book and write the report. He's worried his teacher will give him a bad grade. She might even send a note home to his parents.

Talk/Write About It
- What should Andrew have done differently?
- What should Andrew do next time he has a report due? What advice would you give Andrew?

Scholastic News Sticky Situation Cards (1–3 and 4–6) feature challenging scenarios students can relate to—situation cards cover self-awareness, self-management, decision-making, and social awareness. Try some samples here!

DOWNLOAD HERE!

REPAIRING RELATIONSHIPS

All relationships (teacher-student, student-student, teacher-colleague, teacher-family) have the potential for hurt and misunderstanding. When that happens, use the 3A method.

Apologize Say you're sorry. Even if your intent was good and you didn't intend to hurt or harm anyone. Simply say, "I'm sorry" or "I'm sorry we're dealing with this." Don't tack on unhelpful words like, "I'm sorry *if your feelings are hurt,*" which shift the blame onto the other person and minimize their experience.

Acknowledge State the ways in which your actions affected the other person. If you lost your temper in class, you might say something like, "I got loud and yelled, and that might have felt scary to you."

Make Amends Say what you'll do to fix things. For example, "Let's take a quick break to calm down and stretch a bit." You can also add, "The next time I start feeling frustrated, I'll pause, take a deep breath, and quietly count to 10 before I speak."

You may find it helpful to use the 3A method in a restorative talking circle with your students. Start with a check-in, making space to discuss any conflict or harm that occurred. Have students reflect on what happened and work together to identify next steps to resolution (Wynter-Hoyte et al., 2022).

"When I coach two students in an argument, I mostly listen. Each one knows they'll have time to be heard and to come up with a solution together. I want them to do this when I am not around, too! At the end, I remind them that we are all 'ohana' (family) here!"

—KEKE POWELL, second-grade teacher

Nurturing relationships lays a positive foundation for learning. But relationships alone aren't enough—confidence is key to both student success and teacher growth. Let's explore ways to build your students' confidence while strengthening your own.

CONFIDENCE

CONFIDENCE 101

There's a direct link between confidence, competence, and achievement. Children who know from past successes that they can accomplish a task are more likely to persist, to take risks, and to master skills.

Confident students (and teachers) are:

- ✭ **Resilient.** They are willing to reassure themselves and keep trying when the going gets tough.

- ✭ **Motivated.** They have a goal they're working toward and either enjoy the work or are willing to exert energy to get to that goal.

- ✭ **Poised for growth.** They thrive on knowing they'll have more opportunities to be more and do more with each challenge they take on.

And don't forget, confidence can be developed at any age over time, which means those same principles apply to teachers as well!

Did you know...?
Lack of instructional support can deplete confidence and may cause trauma when students are repeatedly expected to perform at levels for which they don't yet have the knowledge base. Addressing academic challenges can boost students' skills and confidence (Morgan et al., 2008; Warmbold-Brann et al., 2017).

"Students want to be heard, but they also want you to push them to be their best selves. So you need to coach them through difficult experiences and hard things."

—GRACE HEARL, sixth-grade teacher

CULTIVATING COMPETENCE & CONFIDENCE

Students develop confidence via experience—by solving problems and succeeding on their own. So give students plenty of opportunities to develop their skills. Here's how:

1 Show the connection between confidence and competence.

Have kids identify skills they've built outside of school that they are proud of (e.g., learning a new game or mastering sports skills, like dribbling, training a pet, and so on). Help them make the connection between practice and success with the skills and strategies you introduce. Go with the motto, "practice makes progress"—and be sure you are asking kids to practice what they have the necessary knowledge and skills training to do!

2 Express belief in their competence.

Let students know you believe they can handle tasks and challenges—and that you're certain they can learn and grow.

3 Set them up for success.

Give students tasks they can handle. Remember: Repeated success builds confidence, so make sure that all students have the opportunity to experience success. Tailor tasks and challenges to students' skill levels—and gradually increase the complexity of tasks as their skills and confidence grow.

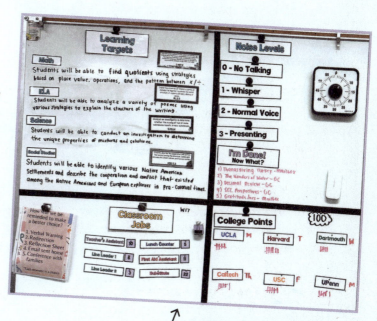

Katie Kim makes efficient use of a board at the front of her room to help her fifth graders monitor and take charge of their learning (she posts learning standards by subject area and assignments for when students have finished the current task) and their behavior (noise-level indicators, classroom job assignments, and their team point system).

4 **Give them clearly defined, meaningful responsibilities beyond academics.**

Kids know the difference between busywork and tasks that genuinely contribute to the success of the classroom. Young children are eager to make valuable contributions, so give them tasks that are essential to helping the class (or school) run smoothly.

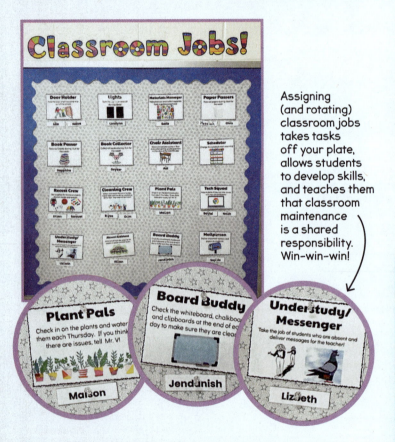

Assigning (and rotating) classroom jobs takes tasks off your plate, allows students to develop skills, and teaches them that classroom maintenance is a shared responsibility. Win-win-win!

5 **Gradually hand over responsibility.**

Use the Gradual Release of Responsibility (GRR) process described in Part 1. At first, you may need to give verbal prompts and reminders. Eventually, students will be able to handle their tasks independently—and be ready to tackle new challenges!

6 **Encourage them to help others.**

As students hone their skills, help them identify ways they can use them to help other people in the class or community. Help them think big! A fourth grader who needs extra practice with fluent reading may be able to do read-alouds for kindergarten students. A second grader who loves building things could help teachers assemble simple classroom furniture.

Check Out This Book!

Make It Relevant!

Elementary specialist Valerie E. King recommends making time for brief student-led, collaborative "learning huddles" with tasks all students can engage with (like solving Rubik's Cubes!) to both build cooperative skills and boost confidence.

Connect & Reflect

Time to get specific! What will you do to boost your students' competence and confidence?

DOWNLOAD HERE!

 FOSTER INDEPENDENCE, BUILD CONFIDENCE

REFLECT: How do you currently foster student independence?

CONNECT: For each step, brainstorm specific activities you can implement.

1 Show the connection between confidence and competence

EXAMPLE: *I will read Peter Reynold's The Dot to my students and discuss how being persistent with something that at first seems scary can lead us to build new skills and create beautiful things.*

I will...

2 Express belief in their competence

EXAMPLE: *I will build in time at the end of the week for each student to share something new they learned or are practicing that they didn't know last week.*

I will...

3 Set them up for success

EXAMPLE: *I will have frequent, short, mixed-skill review practice to ensure that their learning moves into long-term memory. I'll provide small-group or individual reteaching right away for kids who need it.*

I will...

4 Give them clearly defined responsibilities

EXAMPLE: *I will make a how-to anchor chart with photos of my students using center materials correctly and with captions to remind them of the center routines we've learned.*

I will...

5 Gradually hand over responsibility

EXAMPLE: *I will supervise students when they first water plants and show them how to check whether the plant needs more water. As students demonstrate competence, I will allow them to independently water the plants.*

I will...

6 Encourage them to help others

EXAMPLE: *I will teach how to give classmates constructive feedback for their writing using sentence-stem prompts along with our rubric.*

I will...

INDEPENDENCE- AND CONFIDENCE-BUILDING ACTIVITIES

Self-Regulating Cues

Whether you use an SEL program or develop your own strategies for self-regulation, you're probably helping students with examples of positive self-talk. Providing anchor charts or visuals can help students calm their frustrations and work to solve everyday conflicts with their peers.

Alexandra Felix teaches her second graders to solve problems within their control in two steps—and with lots of practice and role-playing. First, the class discusses and categorizes "big" problems (e.g., someone getting hurt or any kind of emergency where an adult is needed) and "small" problems, which can generally be worked out by students themselves (e.g., a friend not taking turns, someone sitting in your chair, or someone who makes you feel excluded during a game—for more scenarios, see Sticky Situations Cards on page 96). Disagreements enrich the conversation, and the class discovers that some problems fit into more of a gray area.

Students learn to ask themselves questions, such as "Am I safe?" and "Can I solve this problem on my own?". They then practice different responses, which they can later choose among by using a problem-solving wheel that is posted in the classroom. Alexandra encourages them to go to the wheel and use it when they need it.

Distinguishing "big" and "small" problems with practice can help students make next-step choices more confidently.

Third-grade teacher Morgan Mercado's calm corner includes a self-reflection mirror where students can focus on themselves and repeat positive "I am…" statements.

Kid-Operated Daily Logistics

With support, older students (and even some younger ones) can manage daily attendance and lunch count. Third-grade teacher Tim Wheeler has delegated those responsibilities to his students and integrated them into their morning routine.

His classroom includes a magnetic board and magnets featuring each student's name. Upon entering, students read the menu choices Tim has posted and move their magnet to indicate their lunch choice: Lunch Choice 1, Lunch Choice 2, or Packed Lunch.

The student who has been tasked with taking attendance counts the magnets after everyone is settled and shares the daily attendance with Tim.

> "Ask, 'What am I doing that students could do for themselves or for the class?'"
>
> —Tim Wheeler, third-grade teacher

Ask Yourself or a Friend

This time-saving strategy encourages students to tap other resources before asking you for help. Here are some cues to give them.

- ⭐ **Ask yourself** Stop and think. What were the directions? What steps can I take to find the answer?

- ⭐ **Look around** Check the classroom environment. What are other students doing? Are there any helpful charts or posters on the wall I can use?

- ⭐ **Ask a friend** Who else nearby could I ask? Together, we can figure it out!

Kids get a big confidence boost when they realize they can solve problems independently—and with their peers.

Try this job application form with older students to incorporate argument-writing skills and help them take ownership of the classroom responsibilities they most want to do.

DOWNLOAD HERE!

Kids Who Resist

Even with great management tools in place, you may have one or more students who exhibit behaviors, like exploding when frustrated or avoiding new activities, that challenge norms or disrupt routines.

These actions can disguise—and distract from—internal struggles and shame. If you think a student needs social-emotional or academic help beyond the support you can provide, make sure you:

1. Ask your mentor or an experienced colleague to observe the student while you teach. If she is watching for disruptive behaviors, for example, she may be able to help you pinpoint the cause of the behavior—as well as elements of your responses that you can change to redirect the behavior.

2. Write down the steps you've taken to address the issue or behavior.

3. Closely observe the behavior over 1–2 weeks. Keep an easy-to-access log to record the date, time, and type of behavior. (For academic challenges, collect work samples and test results.)

4. Share your documentation of behavioral concerns with parents/caregivers and ask for their help in finding a solution. Share the plan you develop with the family and with your coach and/or administrator.

5. If the issue is also academic, work with the learning specialist, coach, or interventionist at your school to identify any assessments to look for areas that might require higher-intensity support. Once the learning needs are identified, the intervention team can work with you and the family to put a comprehensive plan into place for the student.

FRIDAY HOOPS AND CHEERS

Friday afternoons are for shooting hoops in BreAnn Fennell's third-grade classroom.

Right before dismissal, students who have aced their spelling test line up for their chance to toss a ball through the hoop on the back of the classroom door. As each student takes a turn, classmates cheer and clap—"whether they make the shot or not," BreAnn says.

It might look like silly fun, but this class tradition illustrates the power of routines and norms, of effective use of classroom space and time, and of building connections and confidence. It took time for BreAnn to develop this routine, and it will take time for you to discover what works best for you and your class. Experiment and have fun!

BUILDING CONFIDENCE DOS AND DON'TS

DO	DON'T
Give students time to wrestle with new concepts and skills. As they persist, they may discover they're more capable than they thought!	**Over-correct.** If you point out every mistake, student confidence will fade. Select the skill that will provide the most foundational support for that learner; once that is learned and celebrated, move on to the next challenge.
Celebrate success (even small wins!). Build confidence one step at a time. Leverage successes and, whenever possible, celebrate mistakes as learning opportunities (see page 81 for brain-changing language to use).	**Dwell on mistakes.** Mistakes are part of learning!
Build on student strengths. Help students figure out how to use their existing strengths as they tackle new activities. Got a reluctant writer who loves video games? Encourage them to write a story about their favorite video game character—or to imagine and write about a new game.	**Focus solely on weaknesses.** Concentrating your effort on what students *can't* yet do can lead to discouragement and disengagement.
Give students an active role. Confidence is best developed via *doing*.	**Do too much for students.** Whenever possible, let students figure things out for themselves.
Offer specific positive feedback. Pointing out exactly what students did well reinforces their strengths and builds confidence.	**Over-praise.** After a while, "good job!" becomes meaningless.
Ensure every student has opportunities to succeed. Children who experience success feel more confident when facing new challenges.	**Overlook quieter students or compare students to one another.** Everyone is capable and benefits from positive acknowledgment.

CONFIDENCE BUILDING

Dealing With Your Own Stress and Anxiety

There's no way around it: Teaching is a stressful job. To thrive as a teacher, you have to find ways to manage stress and anxiety, both in high-stress moments and over the long haul. These tips for managing high-stress moments can help:

- **Buddy up** Form a pact with a fellow teacher to cover each other's classes as needed. If you feel a panic attack coming on, call your buddy. If they need a break or emergency time-out, return the favor.

- **Step away** If possible, retreat to a quiet space (or head outside—nature is soothing!). If that's not possible, use the Calm Corner in your classroom. You're setting a great example for your students!

- **Acknowledge and deal with your emotions** "Early on in my career, I'd try to be so patient, so calm. I'd push my frustration down, but then it became like a sprint instead of a marathon for me—I felt like I had to sprint through the day before I could release my emotions," says Kevin Frederick, a veteran first-grade teacher. He's since learned that it's better to cope with emotions as they arise, using techniques like deep breathing or taking short breaks.

REALITY CHECK

You don't have unlimited time or unlimited resources. And you're not an expert teacher. So expecting perfection from yourself is a bit unrealistic, don't you think?

Unrealistic expectations—and your inability to meet them—can eat away at your self-confidence. When you feel self-doubt creeping in and spiraling out of control, remember:

Regularly acknowledge your accomplishments (as you do for your students!) and reach out to your mentors and co-workers for support.

Just like your students, you're learning and growing every day.

"I think a lot of teachers come out of teacher prep programs expecting to be 100 percent ready, but that's unrealistic. Don't put yourself down. Remember, you will learn so much in your first five years!"

—KEVIN FREDERICK, first-grade teacher

Long-Term Stress Management

✳ **Routine and regular self-care** It's easy to let self-care slip, especially during busy or stressful times. But that's when you need to lean into self-care. (For ideas, go back to Routines and Healthy Habits in Part 1.)

✳ **Limit negativity** Venting to coworkers can be a great way to release frustration. But doing so constantly is a pure energy drain. Stay curious, ask for help, and spend more time with problem-solvers than with complainers.

✳ **Seek support** As stress levels—and self-doubt—arise, you may find yourself pulling away from your co-workers and friends. Resist that urge. Instead, reach out to people who can help you recharge. If your confidence is seriously flagging—or you're contemplating leaving teaching—it's crucial to ask for advice, perspective, and professional guidance from trusted mentors and administrators.

For Mental Health Support

✳ **Employee Assistance Program (EAP)** Most schools offer programs that give employees access to free and confidential assessments, short-term counseling, referrals, and follow-up services. Your employee handbook or website may have details. You can call or email your HR department for info, too.

✳ **Professional counseling** Therapists can offer tailored strategies for managing stress and building resilience. Check your insurance plan to see which providers and services are covered.

✳ **988 Lifeline** For mental health crises, call or text 988 for immediate, free, and confidential help from trained crisis counselors.

Did you know...?
Education is #18 on the list of professions with the highest rates of alcohol abuse, with almost 5% of educators reporting heavy alcohol use (Bush & Lipari, 2015). A drink here and there is fine, but drinking to cope with stress can quickly become problematic. If you're worried about your drinking, you can call 1-800-662-HELP, SAMHSA's National Helpline.

"If you've ever 'thought about therapy,' just go. Working with a therapist over the years has really helped me."

—TIM WHEELER,
third-grade teacher

Connect & Reflect

Reviewing your accomplishments regularly is a great way to not only recognize your professional growth, but to also boost your confidence. Use these prompts to celebrate your successes.

DOWNLOAD HERE!

 ## CELEBRATE SUCCESS: A CONFIDENCE-BUILDING ACTIVITY

REFLECT	Consider adding these reflections to your calendar, so you don't forget to stop and take stock. Or start a notebook to track your achievements and note positive feedback.
Today:	One thing I did well today is...
This week:	A moment this week when I felt successful was...
This month:	I made progress this month when I...
This quarter/ semester:	One major accomplishment I'm proud of is...
CONNECT	You can use this activity with your class, too! Encourage students to reflect together—and to note their classmates' accomplishments. Celebrating successes together is a powerful way to build confidence and community.

CONNECTIONS & CONFIDENCE SEND-OFF

Ideally, you've landed on a few new ideas for building relationships and boosting confidence—students' and your own! This is what really brings the heart and purpose into classroom management.

Big Ideas to Keep in Mind

⭐ Don't underestimate how much solid relationships will boost positive behavior. Kids thrive when they know they're being led by someone who gets them and are surrounded by classmates who accept them.

⭐ Weave activities and routines into your day that help kids feel more connected to school.

⭐ Develop a network of positive, supportive colleagues to help you manage challenging situations and behaviors—and provide needed reality checks!

⭐ The way you say it matters! Choose words wisely and listen to teachers you admire for ways to spark students' willingness to connect, learn, and take risks.

⭐ Watch for students who say (or show) that they "don't care"—they are signaling that they may need extra support.

⭐ Your role in building kids' confidence goes beyond encouragement. Make sure to regularly monitor progress, teach necessary skills, and celebrate successes!

Alexandra Felix leaves us with this thought: "Connecting with your students is worth every ounce of effort: Knowing and trusting you and their peers is essential to their learning and it helps to create a welcoming environment. I've discovered that you can make space for students' lives in every part of the day—from morning routines to lessons."

Whose voice matters? YOURS MINE OURS!

DOWNLOAD HERE!

Here's a quote you can display to spark discussion with students about the importance of being heard.

REFERENCES

American Institutes for Research. (2020, July). Personalizing student learning with station rotation: A descriptive study. Overdeck Family Foundation.

Archer, A. L., & Hughes, C. A. (2010). *Explicit instruction: Effective and efficient teaching.* The Guilford Press.

Aspirilia, T., Purba, F., & Qodariah, L. (2020). First grader's attention span during in-class activity. *GUIDENA Jurnal Ilmu Pendidikan Psikologi Bimbingan dan Konseling, 10*(2), 144–150.

Barrett, P., Davies, F., Zhang, Y., & Barrett, L. (2015). The impact of classroom design on pupils' learning: Final results of a holistic, multi-level analysis. *Building and Environment, 89,* 118–133.

Bear, G. G., & Minke, K. M. (2018). *Helping handouts: Supporting students at school and home.* National Association of School Psychologists.

Buch, E. R., Claudino, L., Quentin, R., Bonstrup, M., & Cohen, L. G. (2021). Consolidation of human skill linked to waking hippocampo-neocortical replay. *Cell Reports, 35*(10), 109193.

Bush, D. M., & Lipari, R. N. (2015, April 16). *Substance use and substance use disorder by industry.* SAMHSA.

Caldarella, P., Larsen, R. A. A., Williams, L., Downs, K. R., Wills, H. P., & Wehby, J. H. (2020). Effects of teachers' praise-to-reprimand ratios on elementary students' on-task behaviour. *Educational Psychology, 40*(10), 1306–1322.

CDC. (2022). What can schools do? School connectedness. *Adolescent and School Health.*

Craig, H. (2019, Feb 21). 5 positive reinforcement activities to use in the classroom. *Positive Psychology.*

DaSilva, M. (2023). The power of routines in the classroom [white paper]. Western University, Canada. www.uwo.ca/fhs//lwm/teaching/dld2_2023_24/DaSilva_DLD22023.pdf

Fisher, D., & Frey, N. (2015). *Engaging the adolescent learner: Setting the stage for 21st-century learning.* International Literacy Association.

Fisher, D., Frey, N., & Hattie, J. (2020). *The distance learning playbook, grades K–12: Teaching for engagement and impact in any setting.* Corwin.

Godwin, K. E., Almeda, M. V., Seltman, H., Kai, S., Skerbetz, M. D., Baker, R. S., & Fisher, A. V. (2016). Off-task behavior in elementary school children. *Learning and Instruction, 44,* 128–143.

Greene, R. (2010, Sept 10). *Kids do well if they can* [video]. YouTube. www.youtube.com/watch?v=jvzQQDfAL-Q

Hawkins, J. D., Guo, J., Hill, K. G., Battin-Pearson, S., & Abbott, R. D. (2001). Long-term effects of the Seattle Social Development intervention on school bonding trajectories. *Applied Developmental Science, 5*(4), 225–236.

Hubbard, F. (2023, August 17). *How teachers can build professional relationships with each other—and themselves.* Teach. Learn. Grow. The Education Blog.

IRS. (2024, August 21). *IRS reminder for schoolteachers: Up to $300 in classroom expenses deductible for 2024.* News Release.

Kearney, W. S., Smith, P. A., & Maika, S. (2014). Examining the impact of classroom engagement: A multilevel analysis. *Journal of School Public Relations, 35*(1), 80–102.

Kraft, M. A., & Dougherty, S. M. (2012). The effect of teacher-family communication on student engagement: Evidence from a randomized field experiment. *Journal of Research on Educational Effectiveness, 6*(3), 199–222.

Li, J., & Julian, M. M. (2012). Developmental relationships as the active ingredient: A unifying working hypothesis of "what works" across intervention settings. *American Journal of Orthopsychiatry, 82*(2), 157–166.

Lindemann-Matthies, P., Benkowitz, D., & Hellinger, F. (2021). Associations between the naturalness of window and interior classroom views, subjective well-being of primary school children and their performance in an attention and concentration test. *Landscape and Urban Planning, 214,* 104146.

Mapp, K. L., Henderson, A. T., Cuevas, S., Franco, M. C., & Ewert, S. (2022). *Everyone wins! The evidence for family-school partnerships & implication for practice.* Scholastic.

Martin, R., & Wilkins, J. (2021). Creating visually appropriate classroom environment for students with autism spectrum disorder. *Intervention in School and Clinic, 57*(3), 176–181.

Mayo Clinic. (2023, August 16). *Tips for drinking more water.* Speaking of Health: Mayo Clinic Health System.

Morgan, P. L., Farkas, G., Tufis, P. A., & Sperling, R. A. (2008). Are reading and behavior problems risk factors for each other? *Journal of Learning Disabilities, 41*(5), 417–436.

NCES. (2003–04). *Schools and staffing survey (SASS).* National Center for Education Statistics.

NCTQ. (2020). *Classroom management.* National Council on Teacher Quality.

Salloum, S. J., Goddard, R. D., & Berebitsky, D. (2018). Resources, learning, and policy: The relative effects of social and financial capital on student learning in schools. *Journal of Education for Students Placed at Risk (JESPAR), 23*(4) 281–303.

Scott, L. H. (2025). *The words that shape us: The science-based power of teacher language.* Scholastic.

Simon, A. J., Gallen, C. L., Ziegler, D. A., Mishra, J., Marco, E. J., Anguera, J. A., & Gazzaley, A. (2023). Quantifying attention span across the lifespan. *Frontiers in Cognition, 2.*

Steiner, E. D., Woo, A., & Doan, S. (2023, September 12). *All work and no pay—Teachers' perceptions of their pay and hours worked.* Rand.

Thomas, J. (2019, July 11). Group punishment doesn't fix behavior—it just makes kids hate school. *The Conversation.*

Warmbold-Brann, K., Burns, M. K., Preast, J. L., Taylor, C. N., & Aguilar, L. N. (2017). Meta-analysis of the effects of academic interventions and modifications on student behavior outcomes. *School Psychology Quarterly, 32*(3), 291–305.

Wilkins N. J., Verlenden, J. M. V., Szucs, L. E., & Johns, M. M. (2023). Classroom management and facilitation approaches that promote school connectedness. *Journal of School Health, 93*(7), 582–593.

Williams, C. (2021, October 21). *Classroom management: Positive reinforcement.* Center for Student Achievement Solutions.

Wynter-Hoyte, K., Braden, E., & Myers, M. (2022). *Revolutionary love: Creating a culturally inclusive literacy classroom.* Scholastic.

INDEX